Choosing Conscious Health for a Vibrant Life

To Jason & Jessica,

 I hope you find something you need in here.

 Blessings,

 Kristen K. Wernecke

Kristen K. Wernecke

ISBN: 978-1483941493

*This book is dedicated
to my precious son Eli
whom I love dearly.*

Table of Contents

Table of Questions for Readers and Resource List

Acknowledgements

With deepest gratitude I want to thank my husband Tom for all his support during the writing of this book, especially for being with Eli and "holding down the fort" so I could go away and write. I also give deep thanks to my father Harry and my mother Edith, to my sisters Susan and Sandy, to Teresa and to my extended family including Stephanie, Cisela and my husband's family, especially Norma. My roots were strong incentive for writing this book and I am grateful for all I have learned and continue to learn about living well.

I am deeply grateful for the nurturance, support in meals and spirit, and peaceful space that was given by the nuns at Clare's Well, Carol, Jan, and Paula as I wrote in silence and received everything I needed to be at my best. I also want to give deep thanks to my sister Sandy and her husband Fred for their generosity in giving me a space in their beautiful home at their Inn at Sacred Clay Farm so that I could get away to another serene and peaceful place to put my words down on paper. Your support has meant so much to me in creating this book!

To all my clients — I honor and thank you. You are my inspiration for creating this book. Thank you for trusting me and allowing me (in many cases) to know you very deeply, to walk with you through some amazing journeys, to witness the array of feelings, the challenges, the miracles with you, and for giving me the chance to grow with you. This book would not be in the world if it had not been for you – my greatest of teachers. May you all be blessed as you continue walking this earth.

I express my heartfelt gratitude for all those who directly or indirectly contributed to this book. Thank you to my many teachers including Renee Brown, Shelli Stanger-Nelson, Rosalyn Bruyere, Chun Yi Lin, and a very special thanks to Ron Moor, whose heartful and grounded presence has given me the space to become a worthy healer. I also want to acknowledge the many healing practitioners that I have known and worked with over the years. Your gifts have helped shape my own health, my knowledge of healing practices and my ability to practice bodywork. Thanks to all of you, with special mentions to Nancy Graden, Chris Hafner, Ginger Dunivan, Bill Torvund, Chris Gordon, Ned Holle, Sally Cossellius, Dianne Hansen, Angel Phillips, and Jeff Grundtner. May we all continue to blossom and grow through knowing and helping one another.

Thank you to my readers Jessica, Fred, Vickie and Ginger. Your supportive words meant a lot to me, helping me acknowledge that this book is actually quite meaningful to others.

And lastly, I wish to express my immense gratitude to my fabulous writing coach Patricia Francisco who believed in me from the very start and got only more encouraging as we went along on this journey. I truly could not have created this book without your abundant wisdom, your tempered reason when I wanted to resist, and your loving presence throughout. You are such a wonderful teacher and a beautiful person!! Thank you from the bottom of my heart.

Preface

This book is for those who have been thinking about making changes in their lifestyle so that they can feel better on many levels. Good health is not always available without some effort on our part. My hope for you in reading this book is that as you become healthier, you will learn to experience your life as it is happening in a deeper, more fulfilling way. As you learn new things about yourself, find fresh insights and become more accepting and loving of yourself, there is no doubt that you will experience your health and possibly your entire life differently. To be here on this planet and really notice the goodness that is here for you and the gifts that are yours if you choose to acknowledge them, this is a good life. The most important moments of my life have been when I have gone to the depths of my soul or have gone with someone else on a journey to the depths of their soul. This is where the richness is, the real thing.

I am writing this book for all the people who want to make a real change in their overall health. It is for the people who until now have not paid much attention to their health, but they are getting a wake-up call as they age. It is for those people who have realized that what they have been doing for self-care is no longer working. I'm writing for those who are frustrated with the answers they've been given from our present health care system, for those who have negative thoughts towards themselves or their health, and for those who really want to work with these challenging patterns but aren't sure how to go about it. Even people who are maintaining good health now will benefit from the information in this book as they learn about new aspects of health and deepen them into solid lifelong health habits.

The purpose of this book is to help you understand that your health, or lack of health, is something over which you have a lot of control. If you choose, you can begin to adopt healthy habits into your daily life that can immediately help you feel better. Even if it takes a longer time to feel better, it is probably preferable to feeling as if you are becoming less and less healthy every day. This can be simple, but it is not easy. Any change requires desire, determination and perseverance, but the benefits are so great, once you get started and feel the connection with your body, you will find the payoffs are worth the effort. Feeling good physically will help you feel better mentally and emotionally too. You will have more energy to do the things you want and need to do, and to feel like you're really living and appreciating life. I believe this is possible as it is true in my own life and in many others I see around me.

I feel my life is a gift, and that includes my health. It is my desire to be consciously involved in shaping all aspects of my health that are possible to shape. This book will show you just how many areas you really can affect so that you can start feeling better soon. It all begins with being conscious of your current thoughts, beliefs, habits and patterns around your present health. Before you can change anything, you have to know what it is that's not working for you and learn new ways of living and being in the world.

I do not have all the answers. And nobody knows you better than you know yourself. So I encourage you to see the information in this book as an offering. Some ideas may resonate with you; some ideas you may find completely foreign or too far out of your comfort zone (at least for now). Some suggestions may feel totally right for you, and excite you, and help you see yourself and the truth that is yours in a completely new way. My hope is that you learn things about yourself that allow you to break free from anything that keeps you from being a whole and integrated, healthy person. And if that sounds too lofty or difficult, I wish for you all that you choose for yourself. Sometimes all we need to get started, or to continue on our current path, is new information to create new insights. New insights will give us a jumpstart on what we desire and deserve in our lives.

Chapter 1

How I Got Here

Growing up in my family of origin there was a substantial focus on health. So my interest and curiosity to learn about this topic come naturally to me. When I was young, my best friend often said my parents were "health nuts." We ate healthier food than most people, lots of veggies and fruits that my mom soaked in her diluted Clorox bleach solution to take off the pesticides, long before anyone was talking about organic foods; we never drank pop (only ginger ale when our tummies were nauseous), very rarely had sugared cereals, and my mom shopped at the first food coop in the Twin Cities when I was three years old. She even put in her time there as a member, often cutting cheese, or bagging nuts or other foods. We ate balanced home-cooked meals most nights as a family together. We hardly ever had desert because sugar just wasn't a part of our diet. Nobody in our family drank alcohol as I grew up, as my dad's grandfather had been an alcoholic and was shunned from his family for it. A person could say we were purists from a diet standpoint. I have come to see how lucky I was to have such healthy training as a child, which really set me up to have healthy habits throughout my life.

Back in the mid-sixties, we had a family membership to the Sports and Health Club, where my parents worked out, and my sisters and I messed around on the equipment and mostly swam in the pool. My father went running nearly every night after work, for stress relief. Our family liked to go canoeing or hiking or cross-country skiing. And as a child, I was always running around outside whenever possible. I can see now we are all very kinesthetic people and come by it naturally. As a hospital administrator, my father even had someone make him a standing desk, an idea whose wisdom has just recently been confirmed by researchers. As it is, most of my life's work has been standing at a massage table, and I would have it no other way.

My perspective on the world comes partly from two parents who were "different" from the mainstream world we grew up in. I've always thought they were a little ahead of their time. In addition to their eating and exercise habits for instance, my mother chose natural childbirth in 1956, 1959, and 1962. Not only that, my father was present at all of the births, which also was unusual in those years. Most women were highly medicated with no memory of their baby's births, while their husbands sat in the waiting room (or the nearby bar), until it was all over. So my propensity toward thinking "differently" is normal to me, and my path has led me deeper into it than either of my parents.

My parents took us all to family counseling when I was five, for which I credit them, as their marriage was on the rocks. They eventually divorced when I was ten, and my father raised three girls as a single parent in 1972. Nobody else I knew lived only with their dad. But it was from this wounded place that I began my journey toward healing on all levels: mental, emotional, physical and spiritual. It has been a challenging, satisfying and beautiful journey that has given me wisdom that I can share with others.

Let me briefly tell you what I've been doing for the last 30 years. I received a BA, double majoring in psychology and social work. I thought I was going to be a psychotherapist some day because I was extremely interested in what made people tick. For a couple of years I worked in group homes with delinquent teens that were court ordered to be there. It was the hardest job I ever had, extremely stressful and very low paid. I decided to work for a real estate company just to be around adults who didn't swear at me for a while, while I figured out what to do next.

Then came my car accident in 1988 (which I will speak about in more detail later) that changed my life, and ultimately brought me into the Healing Arts. After two years of healing, I started massage school because I was amazed at the positive difference massage had made in the healing of my injuries and even the emotional and mental/psychological healing it brought about. I began working as a massage therapist in Minneapolis in 1990. I loved it, but didn't love my workplace in a salon because of the noisy and smelly environment and lack of freedom. So after six months, I went out on my own, and have worked for myself ever since. During the first few years of being a massage therapist, I also worked at a health food store, which was a great education for me. I learned about Western and Chinese herbs and supplements, and which ones to use for certain maladies. I learned about homeopathy, Bach flower essences, fasting and cleanses, and all of the other interesting things in the store that were used for healing.

In January 1991, I began taking classes from Rev. Ronald Moor at the Center for Wholeness in Minneapolis. He is a teacher of Hands-on-Healing who was trained by Rev. Rosalyn Bruyere, one of the pioneering energy healers in the country. Rosalyn is world-renowned for her research, healing and teaching on energy healing. Using her skills in perceiving and interpreting auric phenomenon, she was instrumental in research conducted at UCLA with Dr. Valerie Hunt, in which the existence and significance of the human aura was first measured scientifically.

The many names for Energy Healing include Hands-on-Healing, Energy Work, Bio-Energy Healing, Healing Touch, Spiritual Healing and Therapeutic Touch. What these terms mean in their simplest form is that practitioners use their hands on or off the body to strengthen, balance and modulate the body's energy field, chakras and meridians. This creates wholeness where there is imbalance, injury or pain. Our human energy system is a three-fold system that includes the energy field (sometimes called auric field or biofield) that surrounds our body; the chakras which are the energy centers inside the body; and the meridians, which form the electromagnetic circuitry for the whole system. I will go into more detail on these terms later in a chapter called "Energy and Healing."

I trained with both Ron and Rosalyn during the next four years, becoming an ordained Interfaith Minister of Healing through Ron's program. I added energy work to my massage therapy practice, and continued to learn more about it and other healing modalities. I have completed three of the five levels of Healing Touch training, and studied Chi Gung with Master Chunyi Lin, Cranio-Sacral training with the Upledger Institute, psychic development with Renee Brown, EFT (Emotional Freedom Technique) with founder Gary Craig, and taken classes with energy healer and teacher Shelli Stanger-Nelson. (Shelli opened a Healing Sciences school called Rhukah Academy in 2010 here in Minneapolis where a person can become a licensed Energy Medicine Science professional.)

For the past 13 years, I have been doing energy healing on people before and after surgery. It helps prepare the body for surgery and helps the body heal more quickly after surgery, and in many cases, with less pain. I have really enjoyed these experiences, and have become quite comfortable working in hospitals, especially after working on my niece at the Mayo Clinic after her motorcycle accident in 2006. (I will go into this in more detail in the chapter called "Freda's Story.") A year after her accident I spoke at the Mayo Clinic about the energy healing I did with her during their annual Traumatic Brain Injury Conference. It was a great experience to speak to 350 speech, occupational and physical therapists about the therapeutic aspects of energy healing. The Mayo Clinic has begun to use integrative therapies to work together with Western medicine technologies and techniques to improve their patients' recoveries. In the months after my niece was in the Pediatric

Intensive Care Ward at Mayo, they hired a full-time massage therapist for that ward.

I have always been extremely interested in the body from various perspectives. I spend a lot of time reading about anything having to do with bodies and healing them. Most of my books fit into some category of mind, body or spirit healing. This has been my passion since I was very young, and everything I learn I try to use in my healing practice as well as in my own journey of health and healing. (I have also learned a lot from my sister who is a nurse, as well as from being in the hospitals and asking questions of the staff, and just from seeing patients in many different medical situations.) Hospitals are using the most amazing technologies now, and my curiosity allows me to learn things many people would never be interested in, but I love learning about the body and how adaptive it can be. The ability of the body to find its equilibrium after traumas large and small continues to amaze me. *We have such brilliantly designed intelligence within our bodies that shows up whenever it is needed. Our bodies will keep on pushing toward life, toward healing and balance until they absolutely cannot any more.*

In addition to my therapeutic massage and energy healing practice, I have been teaching meditation for more than eight years. I teach several classes including a Grounding Meditation class, a consciousness-raising class called Your Healing Journey, and beginning energy healing. Teaching and doing bodywork have been true blessings in my life. It is wonderful to do work that I love and that helps people move toward their optimum health and balance in body, mind and spirit.

My life has given me a meaningful collaboration of experiences and information that assist me as a healer and teacher. They have brought me to this moment and have formed me into a person who is open to possibilities, who believes that the mysteries and miracles that are all around us, are part of something bigger than what is visible to us.

A New Philosophy

If we are going to create real changes in our own health and the health of our country, I believe we first need to look at how we view health challenges and how we respond to them. For many, our health challenges get ignored or medicated until they become bigger problems with a more expensive solution. If we could work with our health issues earlier on we may be able to ward off more serious illness. The perception of health and healing that some doctors have may also be a part of the problem. I am advocating using the mind, body and spirit of the patient as the solution to their physical imbalance or disease.

In my bodywork practice over the last 22 years, over and over I have heard people say they have this problem or that problem. The doctor told them (often years or even decades before) that they have problems like carpal tunnel syndrome, or fibromyalgia, or irritable bowel syndrome and that they will always have that problem. I cringe every time I hear this because it is not true that just because you have that problem at the time a doctor diagnoses it that you will have it for the rest of your life. I am aware of the power that a doctor's beliefs and attitudes around the process of disease can have on the patient. The information patients receive can have a huge effect on the patient's ability to recover. In fact research has shown that the words a doctor uses have a clear impact on how patients relate to their "illness" and their ability to have a positive or negative health outcome.

I am not saying that physical problems don't exist. My concern is with the way so many doctors make a diagnosis, and then focus only on how they can alleviate symptoms. We have become a country way too dependent on prescriptive medications that come with their own long list of side effects. What I am curious about is what made the body weaken or become imbalanced enough to cause a physical problem in the first place. WHY are these symptoms arising?

The body has its own wisdom and its own way of communicating and sharing that wisdom with us. Focusing on getting rid of symptoms amounts to trying to silence that wisdom and ignore its guidance. When we honor the wisdom of our symptoms, it becomes possible to not only alleviate discomfort, but also to restore balance and proper function. We can then prevent a repetition or escalation of the problem. Symptoms are the first signal that dis-ease may be coming on. (The word *disease* means "not with ease" – which could be interpreted as off or out of balance. Throughout this book I will sometimes spell it as dis-ease to emphasize this idea of the body not being at ease and instead being out of balance. This also gives us more space for the idea of returning to balance instead of becoming panicked by being diagnosed with a disease.) For me, listening to and looking for the underlying cause of these symptoms holds the most information and the most power.

If we are going to heal ourselves, we need to have some belief that healing is possible. Saying that someone will have a particular condition for the rest of their life does not give any power to the patient. My hope is that in the future more physicians will converse with patients in ways that include their entire being, going back to the holistic approach that has been lost in Western medicine. This could help patients deal more effectively with their condition and bring them into a proactive way of seeing their treatment or the creation of new habits.

In the next chapter we will learn about how our bodies are like a river that continues to flow in new ways all of the time. This is one of the reasons I believe in a body's ability to heal. My experience tells me that we can heal many imbalances when we give our bodies the proper support, especially since we are creating new cells all the time. With the proper environment, the intelligence of the cell can again create a healthy cell, instead of a cancerous one or an otherwise diseased cell. (This idea has been supported recently by cancer researchers who have become interested in what environment cancer cells can and cannot grow in. This is very new research, and it provides a reason why there are many miraculous cures for cancer in people who completely change their "terrain" so their cancer cells cannot survive.)

By changing our habits we can create a supportive, healing

environment for the body. Changing our diet so the body's chemistry is not one in which cancer can grow or in which other malfunctions take place is one aspect. Regularly moving our body is necessary for the proper functioning of all our muscles, organs, etc. Positive practices in the mind and spirit, like a healthy psychology and using affirmations, meditation and prayer, can also affect the physical body and move it toward healing. I have seen this happen in my own practice with others and in my own body. And I have personally experienced instances of healing of both minor and major ailments that cannot be explained by the current medical model. Think of all the ailments we could help heal in ourselves, given the proper education and belief that it's possible! I intend to give you the tools to do just that.

Chapter 2

How to Begin

Our Body is Like a River

When I was 26 years old, I read Deepak Chopra's bestseller *Quantum Healing - Exploring the Frontiers of Mind/Body Medicine*. Dr. Chopra is an endocrinologist trained both in India and the United States, so he takes the best from Eastern and Western philosophies on medicine. He is a very wise man and prolific writer, with at least fifty-five books addressing various mind, body and spirit themes. In *Quantum Healing* I found something most fascinating that has stayed with me all these years. He wrote that our body is like a river that shifts and changes all the time, constantly making new cells of all kinds. He says that 98% of the atoms in our body are made anew each year. Did you know that your skin is new every month? Or that you have a new stomach lining every four days, and a new liver every six weeks? We also acquire a new skeleton every 3 months, as atoms pass freely back and forth through the cell walls, while the configuration of bone cells remain fairly constant. That has always fascinated me. To me this means that it may be possible to create healthy cells in the place of diseased, unhealthy cells. The science of psychoneuroimmunology speaks to this possibility and is based on the premise that the functioning of our immune system is linked to our thoughts and emotions. (This will be covered more thoroughly in Chapter 8 "Solutions for a Healthier Lifestyle: The Mind/Body Connection.") This premise brings power and hope to the idea that we do, indeed, have the ability to facilitate our own healing process in a conscious manner.

Dr. Chopra also talks about the cells in our body having intelligence. Every cell, whether a liver cell, lung cell, or a kidney cell, has its own knowledge and "talks" to the rest of the body. Because of the complexity of a human body's function, each cell needs to correlate its message with trillions of other cells that are all working at once, along with constant chemical conversation (or exchanges). It cannot be said that there are accidental or unnecessary parts of this intelligence. All of this intelligence is needed to rebuild and continue the flow and change that occurs every moment in our cells and body.

In the case of autoimmune disorders and cancer, the intelligence of the cells becomes confused for some reason, and the body attacks its own tissue in the former, and aggressively creates dangerous cells in the latter. The question is how and why did the malfunction get started?

So let's go back to how the body is like a river. Let's hypothesize that there are three possible perspectives or belief systems we can hold about our body and our health, each with its own kind of response to body symptoms. Let's start with the presumption that you wake up one day with a small but unusual pain in your stomach. We choose one of these three ways to deal with this small pain.

1) **Fearful** - From this perspective, you might feel afraid and immediately call the doctor to see "what is wrong," making an assumption that the pain means there is something wrong with your body that needs outward intervention as opposed to within.

2) **In Denial** - From this perspective, you would ignore or deny the pain and make an attempt to completely forget about it.

3) **Body as Friend** - A third possible response would be to notice the pain, make a conscious note of it, and mindfully pay attention to it over the next few days. In this last example, your internal response is, "hmm, something different is going on; I'm going to keep an eye on it to see if it resolves itself."

These three perspectives themselves can dramatically affect our daily responses (or lack of response) to our bodies and certainly the outcomes of any health challenges we may be presented with. Let's look at how we may establish these different perspectives.

1) In the fear-based response, we see our bodies as something to be managed and controlled. We may feel a sense of separation, where things often "go wrong" without any warning, as if this body is not part of "me." It's more like a car we have to take care of. This often subtle or sometimes blatant fear about our bodies can be either conscious or unconscious.

2) The denial response tends to arise when we relate to our body like it's a stranger that we don't really want to see or acknowledge, so we ignore it and hope the pain goes away. Here, we are ill at ease with our own bodies, so it is easier to NOT act on behalf of our bodies' needs because we lack the acknowledgement that our body is actually "us."

I'd like to make a point here that seems related to both the first and second responses. You may not really want to be responsible for how your body got this way, or don't understand the connection between how you treat your body and how it performs. You would rather someone or something else (like a doctor, or a prescription) just took care of it. This illustrates a disconnection with your body.

3) When we treat our bodies as a friend or a loved one, we respond to it by being aware of and comfortable with its processes. We feel at ease acknowledging when something in our body is "off" and then treat it like a friend by helping its unmet needs get addressed. Knowing that our body naturally flows and changes all of the time as new cells create everything anew over and over again may make it easier to have a more relaxed, calm approach to the things that you notice changing in your body. This is its norm. Any sense we have that our bodies are staying the same is an illusion. For example, we constantly have new skin covering our bodies because our body is continually making new skin as the old skin sloughs away. We may not see this happening, but that doesn't mean that it isn't happening. We just don't look under the microscope daily to notice the everyday workings of this extraordinary miracle we call the body.

I've found that much of the time, as I realize my body is constantly changing, most of these occasional small pains go away within a day or two, and I do not feel a sense of worry or panic around this. I understand my "river" is working on something, and it just needs some time to resolve itself. My job is to allow my body to bring itself back into balance naturally. To do this I may give myself more rest at this time. I may also move my body gently with light exercise to help restore the flow of energy to ensure the discomfort isn't just due to stuck or stagnant energy, and to get my lymph system moving.

An important part of having a healthy relationship with your body, and therefore having better health, is to become aware of what kind of relationship you currently have. Choosing this relationship is better than falling into it because it is in the choosing that we become powerful partners with all the parts of ourselves. Most of us who have unhealthy patterns around health have come upon them unconsciously and innocently. Some of us are not inclined to exercise, just because it never became a habit for us when we were children or young adults.

Though people need to move their bodies or exercise to be healthy, we may not have connected our inactivity with not feeling good. If we have no experience with that, how would we know?

Similarly, people don't just go out to eat and purposefully find the dinner with the most fat, calories and sugar as possible, to see how much weight they can gain. Instead they just haven't learned that eating out a lot and surely at fast food places is more likely to bring up health issues over time. Or they just don't care (and therein lies a whole separate conversation). Learning that there is a healthier way to eat that will allow us to maintain a constant body weight and feel good can help change present habits. (I will address this more specifically in Chapter 5 "Solutions for a Healthier Lifestyle: Nutrition, Diet and Consciousness Around Food.")

For many of us, our bodies work quite well for many years without us having to put much effort into caring for them. Then, as we age we wonder why that is not working the same way for us anymore. It can be because we have accumulated problems from years of bad habits and finally we're feeling their effects. Unfortunately it also simply takes more effort to maintain a basic level of health as we age. Having conscious awareness of what we're dealing with is the place to start. When we realize it is in our power to become healthier, we feel more inclined and inspired to work on it. With this book I hope to show you the power that you have to restore your own health and vitality so that you can once again feel good physically, emotionally, mentally and spiritually. You really can do it! (And it's the best gift you could ever give yourself, your children, your spouse and everyone else who loves you.)

What is Consciousness?

First I would like to be clear about what consciousness is for our purposes here. *New World Dictionary* says to be conscious is "1. To have a feeling or a knowledge (of one's own sensations, feelings etc., or of external things); aware; cognizant. 2. An awareness of oneself as a thinking being who knows what one is doing and why. 3. Accompanied by an awareness of what one is thinking, feeling and doing; intentional."

When you are conscious you might say there is a knowing of what is happening inside yourself and around you. Quite often we humans operate from an unconscious place. In fact some people think we're unconscious as much as 93% of the time (scary to think about). Much of what we do is done on automatic pilot, without a conscious effort. Being unconscious in this way is the opposite of being intentional. When someone is being intentional, there is a determination to do a specific thing or act in a specific manner, basically doing something *on purpose*. That is what this book is about. Becoming aware and intentional in our choices around our health helps us take the first step, and all the following steps toward creating health in our lives. It is about living *on purpose.*

Beliefs and Attitudes

As we go through the many stages of our life, we construct a set of beliefs to operate by. Beliefs are ideas that we come to treat as truths, or rules that we live by. Beliefs are thoughts we think over and over again. The more we tell ourselves something, the more true it becomes for us. Our beliefs are what shape our reality and many of us don't ever consider our belief systems in any realm, whether it is about health and wellness or something else. Becoming conscious of our own beliefs and attitudes about our health is the first step toward achieving the optimum health that is possible for our body.

For example, if you have a belief that exercising is hard work, then you are likely to avoid doing it, even though there are many activities that would count as exercise that you might enjoy. If you believe that what you eat does not affect your health or how you feel, you will eat anything that you like to eat. You may find yourself taking over-the-counter drugs or a prescription to get relief from the symptoms of heartburn, bloating or gas, not being aware of the connection between your discomfort and the food you eat. This is how beliefs run our lives. We base our behaviors on beliefs and often these beliefs are unconscious. So our attitudes and behaviors are caused by the beliefs that we sometimes don't even know we have. That's why a person's beliefs and attitudes can seem incongruent at times. For example, some people believe that they will live a very long time, but then they also smoke, as if that won't affect their longevity.

Let me give an example of a belief that I have that has a huge impact on my health and the way I relate to it. My present belief is that I get healthier and feel better as I get older. The reason I have this belief that drives my outlook on health and aging is because of my car accident when I was 25 that changed my life in so many ways. Physically, I went from being an extremely healthy and fit young woman to a person who hurt constantly with soft tissue damage (muscles, ligaments and connective tissue), a spine that twisted in opposite directions at the top and bottom, problems with my organs due to the nerve disruption in my spine and damage to my focusing nerve which affected my vision. This altered my belief system because prior to the accident I had a belief that I could take good care of myself, and maybe even be in full control of my health, and I would be a healthy person. The car accident shattered that belief because I found myself in a painful, difficult situation that changed everything I had previously known about my body because something happened *to me*. Over time and with much effort I have learned that my body keeps improving because I continue to be aware of its limitations and continue to work to improve them.

The car accident required that I do a lot of work to heal my body, and as it turned out, I also had go to the depths of my being to heal my emotional/mental and spiritual parts of myself as well. These parts had all been wrapped together and were shaping my present existence which involved a lot of of pain, depression and exhaustion. My sensitivity as a person made this a really deep process as I worked through these unhealed parts of myself from my childhood. It was necessary though to work simultaneously with the physical and all the other pain together. Ultimately, my present belief formed from this new place of consciousness, and I continue to believe that I become more healthy and whole and continue to improve my overall health of mind, body and spirit as I age.

This is not as clear cut as it used to be, because I can see some signs of aging in myself, but I also feel stronger, healthier and happier at age 50 than I did when I was younger. For most people though, this is the opposite of what they believe. They have been told, or have seen this in older people, and have surrendered to the belief that as they age, their bodies break down and they have more and more pain, and less and less "health" until they die (despite the fact that we are building new cells constantly). The sad part of this kind of thinking is that many of us don't realize that we have a choice about how we age. Every day we make choices that affect how we will feel physically in the future, but many of us are not yet aware that that is the case. (Hence, the bad habits we get into and the self-fulfilling beliefs we hold.)

You may have your own stories that have brought you to your present beliefs around your own health, and they may give you a starting point to see how you choose or don't choose healthy living. As I mentioned, many of the beliefs that we have are unconscious and may also be untrue at this point in our life even if they were once true. This is why it can be helpful to become consciously aware of what beliefs you currently hold on various subjects. For our exploration here we will be focusing on those beliefs that relate to your physical health, and later in the book you will have the opportunity to answer questions that will shed some light on your thoughts and ideas about emotional and spiritual topics related to your health.

Throughout the course of this book there will be a set of questions that goes along with many of the chapters. There are no right or wrong answers. Some of these questions may make you uncomfortable. I really encourage you to stay with them because on the other side of that discomfort are practical answers. The reason for asking the questions is to get you thinking in new and different ways about aspects of your health. Becoming conscious of what your present beliefs and ideas are is the first step in creating any kind of change. My hope is that in learning more about yourself as you read this book you can see the blocks that have kept you from your optimum health, and find the insights that will bring forth new energy to help you create a healthier way of life.

Questions to help you explore your current beliefs that may affect your health

1) Do you believe that as you age you are inherently going to feel worse?

2) Do you think it is possible for you to age and still feel healthy and pain free?

3) Would you be willing to challenge your present belief system when it goes toward negative thoughts around aging?

4) Do you believe that those "other" people who seem to age well just have good genes?

5) Do you have the desire to learn about healthy practices they could share with you?

6) Do you have a health condition that you would like to work with in a different way that might help you feel better?

7) Do you believe that you can affect your health by practicing certain "healthy" behaviors that you haven't tried yet?

8) Are you willing to try some new behaviors to see how you could feel differently?

9) Can you see where your present belief system holds you back from working on health issues?

10) Is there something that happened in the past that gave you a belief that keeps you from working on better health habits now?

11) How could you change a belief or beliefs so that you can feel better now? (Hint: Becoming conscious of that belief is the first step to choosing what is really true now so that you can be free to change your behavior.)

Again, I encourage you to answer these questions and mull over your answers. You may even wish to keep a journal for them, as you will probably learn a lot about yourself and your answers will most likely change over time as you grow in awareness. If you are someone who has been looking for answers to health and wellness questions, answering these questions is a great place to begin. It will help you realize if your relationship with your body is one of friend, adversary or stranger. That is a great place to start with your healing.

So What Do You Think of Your Body?

What you think or believe about your body, say to yourself about your body, and do with your body is of the utmost importance in determining your health and wellness throughout your life. If you believe in your body's own ability to heal, then you will consciously care more for your body. If you don't believe in your body's own ability to heal, you may be less likely to take care of it. If you believe that the actions you take in regard to your health matter, they will more likely make a difference. As I mentioned earlier, some of us consider our body to be a stranger, some a friend and some an enemy or adversary. Where you lie on this spectrum could greatly affect how you heal. The good news is that even if you have been treating your body as an enemy or a stranger, once you become conscious of that attitude you can shift your behaviors toward a more loving relationship with your body.

Questions to help you discern
your current relationship with your body

1) Do you like your body?

2) Do you trust your body to do what you ask of it, to stay healthy if you treat it well, to recover from illness or injury?

3) When you feel pain or an illness do you feel afraid? If so, do you know why?

4) Do you immediately go to the doctor when something is a little off or do you wait and see for a short time?

5) Do you separate yourself from a body part or system that isn't working well at the moment, to the degree that you are angry with it, try to ignore the problem or wish to punish it? (As if that part of your body isn't part of you?)

6) Do you think your body has the ability to heal itself with your support, i.e. getting enough sleep, eating well, exercising, using supplements, etc.?

7) Would you prefer to use a pharmaceutical or surgical approach rather than look for another, possibly less invasive plan of action?

8) Do you give yourself (and body) negative messages around its lack of health?

9) Do you give yourself (and body) positive messages for living a healthy lifestyle or working in that direction?

10) What do you say or think to yourself when you are sick or tired or down?

11) Have you ever purposefully used your mind to heal something in your body?

12) Have you ever meditated or prayed to work with a physical issue or relationship issue?

13) Do you think you have a physical issue at this time that needs help and do you know how to start working with it?

14) Are you geared more toward prevention on health issues, or would you rather take care of illness once you have it?

If you find you treat your body like an adversary (something that opposes you or is even an enemy to you or something to be denied), this is a serious mind/body/spirit split that can only bring you farther away from health. It would be useful to find ways to shift your attitudes and beliefs toward a more hopeful and loving relationship with your body. You may wish to focus on loving your body and appreciating it for all it does for you. You may wish to say something positive to it every day, for example "I am getting stronger every day", or "My body knows exactly what to do", or "I love and appreciate my body just as it is." Your body will hear you.

In fact as I have worked on people's bodies for 22 years, *I have come to believe that bodies think like a four-year-old who is in a good mood. Bodies have an open, receptive quality to them and accept love, hear positive messages with glee, and respond immediately to loving touch, words and intention. Never underestimate a body's ability to find its balance.*

My experience has shown bodies to be absolutely amazing, miraculous works of art. They have so much wisdom and if you tap into that wisdom, you will learn from your body – it has much to say. When faced with a pain in your body, you can ask that part of you what it wants you to know. What message does it have for you? Then listen, and allow your intuition to tune into that part of you and hear what it says. For example, your throat may be sore, but you have no other symptoms of a cold or flu. So you take a quiet moment and ask yourself, "What is this sore throat about?" You may find out that you have been holding in some emotion and some conversation that needs to be expressed to another person. Or it may be that you were shouting at a football game. It can be as simple as that. But if you don't take the time to slow down, go quietly inward, you would never come up with that answer. (And you may go get a cold medication that gives you side effects that you would rather not have.) You might be surprised how much wisdom you can gain about your whole being, by going inside, and with a quiet and receptive quality, just ask a question, like "What do I need right now?"

If you can do what I just mentioned, your body will soon become your friend. Whether you think or believe that your body is a friend or not makes a difference; so it is to your advantage to work toward that if you are not already there. If your body was your friend, would you ignore it? Would you talk negatively to it and criticize it? Would you have no compassion for all the hard work it does for you? Bodies are doing millions of different functions for us at every given moment. They deserve our respect, care, support and kind thoughts if we expect them to continue working hard for us. Generally, I think it is rare for people to consider their bodies in this way. But if we did consider our body as our friend, we would care enough to make the changes that it needs to work optimally for us. We would work *with* our body and its natural ability to heal, not against it.

Thirdly, it is common for people in our culture to have no relationship with their body at all (at least consciously), which I call the stranger position. This belief system is not helpful to our quality of life and it takes away any incentive to make changes for the better. If we don't care enough about something, we will do nothing. The person who has this perspective isn't interested in having awareness or time for things of "the body." They go through life without noticing the physical part of themselves as being something they need to take care of or do anything about. They don't engage in self-care or positive health habits. They usually assume that everything will be okay in their body, until they find out it isn't okay. And then they may feel their body has betrayed them somehow. This is a position of zero power in terms of your health. If you don't even recognize that you are at the ship's helm, then how can you steer the ship? I feel sad for people who have disconnected this much from their bodies, and sometimes this means disconnecting from their spirits as well, both of which tends to make people unhappy. They tend to be "head" people and focus all their attention there. If that is you, ask yourself what makes you afraid about matters of the heart, body or spirit? What started this belief and way of thinking may have happened when you were very young, and it is likely no longer true. Choosing a new belief in this area could change your life. It is safe and healthy to relate to your body with kindness and caring. All parts of you deserve this, and I believe it could really make a difference.

When it comes to healing major physical challenges, I have realized that it is very important to believe in miracles and to have faith and hope as a starting point. Each time I have witnessed small miracles and major miracles along my journey as a healer I feel amazed and so blessed to be a part of people's healing stories. It is because of my witnessing that I hold a deep faith in the ability of people to heal their many ailments from serious disease to chronic pain.

Chapter 3

One Miraculous Healing Story

This is a story about healing serious disease, and it was through this story that I learned to have an open and positive mind when it comes to healing. I was at an impressionable age as I became witness to the healing process of someone close to me. As I watched this person go through her process of healing in unconventional ways, I became curious and learned about some of the modalities that she was working with. I'm sure that this experience opened my mind to different possibilities, and helped set me up for my interest in health and healing as I became an adult.

This is only one person's experience of healing and I am not advocating it as "the way" to heal cancer. Many people can heal cancer by using Western medicine and others choose to incorporate both Western and integrative approaches into their healing plan. We are all entitled to our own process and will respond best to the things that feel right for us. Cisela's path was right for her and luckily, it has given her a huge extension on her life.

It was 1974, and I was 12 years old when my stepsister's mother, Cisela, whom I was close to, had a colonoscopy after experiencing many symptoms of cancer. She had polyps that were removed and tested and she was indeed diagnosed with colon cancer. She was offered chemotherapy, but knew immediately that that would not be right for her, nor did she think it would work. So instead, she set out on her own healing journey that had many layers and processes.

The night of her diagnosis, she was terrified that she would die from the cancer. She had been divorced just months before this diagnosis and was on her own. She talked to God and Jesus, and asked them to "Please show me the way. I want to live for my children [ages 9 and 11] and to love and be loved. I'm willing to surrender to you."

The next evening she was with a friend who asked her if she had heard of natural treatments for working with cancer. This was exactly what she was interested in, as she was not one who would use chemicals to heal her body. Her friend gave her names and phone numbers of people in a group in St. Paul called Cancer Victors and Friends (there was also a national group with this name). She went to the group and spoke with three people who had gotten well after having a cancer diagnosis. She also learned of a doctor in California whom she soon went to for treatment. He was an engineer as well as a medical doctor, and he used a technique called radionics, (other names for the same process are radiesthestia and psychotronics) to help heal imbalances in the body including cancer. This technique is widely used in Europe.

Cisela (who came to the U.S. from Sweden at age 21 to attend Cornell University) worked with this doctor in California. Though she didn't have a liver or pancreas biopsy, she had all of the symptoms of malfunction in those organs (as well as her colon) that usually mean they are cancerous. Many people who have only one of those types of cancer will die, as they all are very serious. But Cisela had faith in the new techniques she was trying, and certainly had the will to live. She continued to use radionics for healing for the next three years.

Next she found someone who checked people for hormonal balance. She found out that her pituitary was underactive and that her thyroid was overactive so she was given a natural hormone to balance it. She went home and realized that she had a **lot** to learn about the workings of her body. She read prodigious amounts of information about bodies and healing and did a lot of soul searching. All of this learning set in motion a huge field of therapies that she continued using to work on her own healing.

She realized that to completely heal, she would have to work with four categories in herself:

1) Physical

2) Emotional

3) Intellectual

4) Spiritual

To do this work it would mean she would need to release and detoxify and then re-activate and rebuild herself on all four of the above levels. This was a process that took years, and for her, it has meant continuing to have a lifestyle that includes being conscious of each of the four levels listed above, even after her cancer was gone. Living healthy became a way of life, a chosen path for her because even after healing the immediate issue, she wanted to maintain a level of health that brought confidence to her that her cancer would not return. Similarly, Bill Moyers says in his book *Healing and the Mind* "Health is not just an absence of illness. It is a way of living."

During her time of crisis, Cisela completely changed her diet for three years. She lived on fruit and vegetables, 80% raw and 20% cooked for two years; plus one quart of fresh pressed carrot juice daily for the first year. During the third year she was able to add basmati rice to her diet. She also did four "Sonne" cleanses for detoxification in the first two years and then continued doing less per year for some time after that. She had many colonics (colon cleanses), used an isolation tank, did Tai Chi and exercised. She also used different herbal supplements as part of her healing, along with homeopathy and Bach flower remedies. These things were meant to reactivate her system once the detoxification had taken place. In addition she received many forms of bodywork, including rolfing, and various forms of energy work like Reiki and some others that she thought were "out there" at first, but they proved to do good things for her.

For her mind, she learned to think positively, to replace limiting thoughts with more healthy ones, and she went to many, many spiritual and mind/body-related conferences for six years. She also continued to do a lot of reading of books and articles related to healing on all levels. She was always prepared to take courses to learn more, or to look at things that weren't working in her life. She had to work with her emotions, learning to express them and transform them through therapy. She did a lot of work looking at and overcoming fears that she had held for many years. There were many wonderful teachers and much to be learned. Her whole life philosophy was "What if I didn't try this and it was the very thing I needed to heal me?"

For a few years she gave speeches and testimonials at spiritual healing conferences. She also learned Reiki healing, and learned to work with a pendulum, a form of radionics for her own healing initially, and later to help others with their healing. Because of the vast amount of information she learned, and because she has always had an international viewpoint and an open mind, it's been my experience that Cisela can find the exact supplement or healing prescription for a person's present issue. When doing a health reading for someone, she has unlimited options to choose from because she has encountered so many different modalities for healing.

During a workshop at the Humanistic School of Business in 1978, Cisela was given another blood test. She had the healthiest, cleanest blood test of all of the seventy to one hundred participants who attended. She had intuitively known already that she was completely healthy and free of her cancer, but it was a lovely feeling knowing it for sure.

Then in 1994 Cisela felt her cancer had come back. She realized this first in a thought form, but then took a test and sure enough, it came back positive. She used diet and herbs to work with the cancer, and it cleared in a short time.

When I think of this story, even now, I am amazed at the strength and resilience of Cisela. She is still alive today, 39 years after her first diagnosis of cancer. Her open mind led her to an alternative path to healing where she was willing to look beyond just the disease she had to the thought forms and behaviors that may have brought it into her body. She remained hopeful as well. Her tenacity and her will and her spirit carried her through a most incredible healing journey that changed her life forever. She is so much more than she was before she found out she had cancer, and it was because of her deeper healing that she was able to shed that dis-ease in her body. Cisela believes that cancer is a spiritual awakening. She believes that its purpose is to wake people up to re-thinking what their life is all about.

I have heard from other cancer survivors, or survivors of other traumas or major difficulties in life, that their disease or whatever it was that challenged them, was a huge gift to them as individuals. Their growth that takes place on all levels and particularly at the spiritual level gives me deep respect for their process. It is in hardship that we can learn about our hidden strengths, our deepest passions, our purpose for being here, and the love that we carry as a beacon of light in this world. In this way we can help the other wounded travelers that cross our path, and offer them the hope and faith we have come to know and believe in.

"A wise man should consider that health is the greatest of human blessings, and learn how by his own thought to derive benefit from his illnesses."

— *Hippocrates*

Chapter 4

American Culture and Lifestyle:
Challenges to Our Health

If you don't feel good it's not necessarily "your fault." But if you aren't satisfied with your health, it *is* your responsibility to find out where your weaknesses are in achieving optimum health and to learn how to strengthen those areas and bring them back into balance and wellness. Your health depends on your own personal participation. This is what I have been learning about and practicing for most of my life, and where I hope I can shed some light for you on your journey toward your definition of "living a healthy life." You deserve to be free of pain and disease, to feel strong and be able to achieve whatever it is that you choose. As my father used to say, "If *you* don't take care of yourself, who will?"

Before we can get to some tools for creating a new, healthier life, I would like to offer my own theory about how Americans have gotten so far away from true health.

Some of the main obstacles to our personal health right now are the cultural ideas and beliefs that have been ingrained in us just by being a part of American society. Many of us have learned that it is a doctor's job to keep us healthy, to have all the answers for us, to give us the right drugs and to save us from whatever disease we may find ourselves suffering from. This medical model's goal is to find a "cure" for a symptom or remove that symptom. I am advocating a different approach because curing is really an external mechanism of providing relief for physical symptoms. This is useful to some degree, but it does not address why or how the body has manifested these symptoms in the first place. This leaves us wide open to contracting more physical problems, since we never looked at the original problem or imbalance in the body. I am more interested in a model for "healing" the body using a multidimensional approach of continually moving toward balance and wholeness, which would include our mental and emotional, spiritual and physical parts of ourselves.

Many of us haven't learned the direct connection between our behaviors, our feelings, and our health issues or the way our bodies work for us. Many of us never learned to pay attention to our own bodies; to feel the subtleties of something that may be off balance before big problems set in. Unfortunately this means many have strayed far away from personal responsibility for their own health and wellness.

For some of us, when we got hurt at a young age we were told to "be tough," "don't worry about it," or other versions of "move on and get over it." In this case we were basically taught NOT TO FEEL. These messages may or may not have helped us at the time, but what they did do quite well was to teach us to ignore and even separate ourselves from our bodily sensations and emotions. After enough years of focusing ourselves on everything but our bodies, we've become habitually conditioned to NOT FEEL emotions or body sensations. Our training and the amount of overstimulation we continually receive as a result of our culture has made many of us numb, afraid and disconnected from ourselves and the world around us. This huge disconnection between body, mind and spirit has happened to us on both an individual and cultural level, and it has also spread to our medical model.

Past cultures had respect for the trinity of mind, body and spirit. They didn't separate health into physical and non-physical components the way that we do. Instead they had a holistic approach to the imbalances that cause health problems and a holistic protocol to move toward health. It is very important for our overall health to be connected to both our physical and non-physical selves. To be able to use our mind and our spirit when our physical health is out of balance or being challenged is an asset. To be able to use our body, when our mind and our spirit have become challenged is also an asset. Calling on our spiritual strength when our physical or emotional strength is ebbing is also beneficial. Each one helps to keep the other two in balance, and gives us more resources with which to deal with any imbalance in our whole health system, which includes all three elements: mind, body and spirit.

Over decades of experience I have begun to suspect that it is the separation of mind, body and spirit that is at the core of our society's lack of health. I would like to help people find new ways to reunite these parts of ourselves that work best together. I believe that bringing back this three-part system, and remembering who we are from a holistic perspective will strengthen our access to vibrant health and vitality.

Lifestyle Changes

Over time, our American lifestyle has changed and evolved into something much different than it was even fifty years ago. These changes have affected our bodies, minds and spirits in so many ways, and unfortunately not all of them have made us healthier. Let us look at our lifestyle as it pertains to health. We hear about nutrition and diet, exercise, sleep, relaxation, smoking, drinking alcohol, meditation, yoga, supplements, herbs and the effects of all these topics. In fact, I think there is an overabundance of information, which is why it can get confusing. My question to you is this: How do you hear this information and what do you do with it, if anything?

Let us start out with general questions that may seem odd to you, but there is a reason for them if you can bear with me.

Questions regarding your health interest and practice

1) Do you think much about your health?

2) Are you a person who is interested in reading articles about healthy living practices, or would you like to be someone who does more than you do now?

3) What are some of the messages that go around in your head about taking in or not taking in what studies have found about health and/or lifestyle practices?

4) Would you prefer to ignore information about healthy practices, and if so why?

5) Do you think it is possible to feel better than you do right now?

6) Are you willing to do whatever it would take to help you become an overall healthier person so you can feel better?

7) What parts would be hardest for you?

8) What parts would be easiest for you?

The purpose of these questions is to gain awareness of how you think and feel about health care practices in general and to see how much personal responsibility you would like to take for your health. I think that people who have thought of their bodies as strangers or adversaries are less likely to have interest in learning about how they could have a healthier lifestyle. Having the willingness and then having the desire to learn about healthy living can move you into a more positive relationship with your body. Those who have stayed away from a positive relationship with their bodies may not be feeling so well. Whether we want a relationship with our bodies or not, we will have one because we have bodies and our bodies are a reflection of us. We do get to choose whether it is a positive or negative relationship and if we choose to become healthier, it would be easier to be in a positive relationship with our body.

A big part of our relationship with our bodies includes the degree to which we have self-love and our ability to practice self-care. (We will discuss this in Chapter 9 later in the book.) As we were growing up, not many parents were talking to us about self-love or self-care. I learned about them both in my twenties, and gratefully they both come easily to me most days. But it was not that way until I did some major work and practiced creating new and healthier habits. Now I usually know what I need and the challenge is fitting it into my time frame with all of the responsibilities I have to my family, my clients, my home, etc. It is easy for us to put ourselves last on the list to receive, but it is a healthy practice to write ourselves in on our calendar so we get to those things we need for ourselves, which will keep us doing our best. Having support from our partners, friends or families will also make this easier.

In the next section we will look at a variety of topics that I have put into the category of lifestyle changes. As we look at them, try to keep in mind the ideas of self-love and self-care. Doing what needs to be done to live a healthier lifestyle will be easier if you feel you are giving yourself the gifts of self-care and doing it out of self-love. In fact, your whole relationship with yourself may change as you go on this journey. For some, this self-care might be a slightly different approach from what you have been doing. For others it could be dramatically different, depending on where you start from and your desires for change. Remember that life IS change, and that change is movement. It need not be feared. YOU are the one steering this ship, and you get to make the decisions about how much or how fast you want to feel better. This is your journey to be created by YOU!

Food

We live in a society of consumerism, commercialism and capitalism. This has turned out to be a destructive combination when it comes to what we eat. I see advertisements telling people to eat a certain kind of food that I know to be very unhealthy, and it really disturbs me. I tend to think that most people have heard that trans-fats, sodium, sugar and other chemicals are going to cause problems in our bodies if we eat too much of them on a regular basis. Still, advertisements continue their push, whether it is something healthy for you or not. Of course, we all get to choose what we eat, but some consumers are not informed on the topic of healthy eating, and they are succumbing to those companies that don't care about consumer health, they just want to sell you their products. I think there is an ethical issue here around withholding honest and complete information for the purpose of making money. Despite federal regulations, we are often left to decipher the messages we see and hear on our own.

Another cultural difficulty that I see has to do with how much our lives have sped up and how this has pinched our time for preparing good, healthy food. Many people grab food on the go, and usually it is not the healthiest of foods. If you choose to do this every day you are getting far less from your food than you could be. Remember this is a choice; nobody's making you buy foods that give you little nutritional value, and it's not about being a good or bad person. Ask yourself what you really want. The first step to making a conscious choice is to look at what you are choosing to eat now and decide if it is in line with your values and goals in this area. If it is not, then you get to decide how you could change it. I know many people, including myself, who avoid fast food, processed foods, or foods full of chemicals. There are plenty of healthy and organic choices out there for you now, if that is what you're looking for.

During the course of writing this book I have spoken with people about cooking healthy meals. What surprised me is that many people have never learned how to cook. I guess because I had a mother who cooked every night and then taught me to cook, I assumed it was the norm, but I stand corrected. To those who never learned how to cook, I recommend taking a simple cooking class or asking a friend to teach you some basics. This can really change your relationship with food and allow you to eat healthier (and possibly cheaper) food. Cooking can be fun and quite easy.

I make a healthy dinner every night for my family with organic food, including vegetables, meat and rice (or a similar whole grain) and it typically takes about 20-25 minutes. Yes, you may have to cook, but the amount of time it takes is not exorbitant. To me it is quite reasonable, and the benefit to your family and yourself is certainly worth the time if eating healthy food is a value for you. It may require you to think ahead but once you get used to doing that as you shop for groceries it becomes second nature. You can plan your family's meals ahead of time and have the food ready for all your meals and snacks that are healthy and really what you want to be eating, so you don't have to grab something less healthy on the road.

One lifestyle choice you may want to make around buying food is doing shorter shopping trips more often, like once or twice a week so that you are getting fresh vegetables, meats, dairy, fruit and whole grains and eating them when they are fresh. This does not necessarily take more time, it just means rearranging your time differently around grocery shopping trips. And yes, while eating organic foods is healthier for your body and for the planet, it does cost more. I realize that not everyone can afford to buy all or even some organic foods. I feel very lucky that I can, but I also know that because of my values it is a priority for me, and even if I have to reduce other expenditures it is worth it to me. When cost is a barrier, investigate exactly what the costs are and choose carefully which foods you can afford to buy organic or "free range" and which you will need to purchase without those labels. Use your common sense. Vegetables are healthier than chips, and protein is necessary whereas dessert or soda are not (and can be very costly). Being conscious here is the key.

With regard to shopping for food, it is also helpful to be an ingredients reader, especially if you are shopping at grocery stores as opposed to food co-ops, or specialty stores known for healthier food alternatives. To eat healthier it is best to steer clear of foods with sugar, corn syrup, hydrogenated oils, trans fats, salt and long lists of ingredients, which usually include a lot of chemicals. As a general rule, the shorter the ingredients list, the better the food will be for you. By just reading the ingredients lists of the foods you currently eat, you may be surprised and become educated about healthier food choices, and it could make it easier to choose healthier foods for you and your family in any store where you shop.

Movement

This is not a chapter on exercise, but rather on the lifestyle that we have created that keeps us from moving, which is different than what human beings had been doing for the last centuries. In the past, we were people that moved each day out of necessity. We had to go get water from a well. We had to go out to the fields and do physical labor to feed ourselves. We had to walk to school throughout all the seasons. We were physical not for exercise purposes, but to survive. These behaviors kept us physically healthier and with fewer chronic diseases, for longer into our lifetimes than many of us experience now.

Of course this has shifted dramatically and quickly during the last fifty to sixty years. Most of us drive to the store to get everything we need. Many of us drive to work and to everything else we do. Most children take buses to school and have very little recess time while at school, and there is less time given to gym class for students as well. This sets up the beginning of bad habits for children who don't get enough movement on a regular basis. Unfortunately for many children that becomes their standard of normal. When many of us were young we played outside almost any time we were not in school, running and playing games, and moving in general. Even in cold weather we would get all bundled up to do some movement outside, while building forts, going skating or sliding, etc. But now these behaviors seem to happen much less frequently and it has led our country into a child and adult obesity epidemic that we didn't have a generation or two ago. The statistics on this topic as of late 2012 report that one third of U.S. children and teens are overweight or obese and two thirds of U.S. adults are overweight or obese. Certainly these numbers need to be recognized and some serious change needs to happen.

Technology has been both a blessing and a curse, and has indeed made it more difficult for children and adults to get enough movement each day. Television has become a huge source of "entertainment" and, may I say, one source for mind, body and spirit numbing. If you spend a lot of time on a computer or with any of the other technological devices we use daily, it takes time from your life for other things. It seems one of the first things to go for many people is exercise or movement. There are several technologies that have been specifically invented to save us time, but they have also led to our decreasing movement in our daily lives, and in many cases increased pollution. I'm thinking of riding lawn mowers, snow-blowers and leaf blowers (a pet peeve of mine, as they are noisy for everyone else around them and don't appear to save time). We like short-cuts, and some of us have the push mower but resort to hiring the kid next door to mow our lawn for us.

Maybe we have become a bit lazy. And I'm not saying all of us, but as a culture it seems to me that many of us don't want to do much physical labor of any kind, and this does not help our physical fitness. We need to recognize that there IS a connection between not moving our bodies and the fact that our country as a whole has become quite sedentary, leading us to the astounding numbers cited above for individuals who are overweight or obese. Being overweight in itself becomes a fertile ground for a lowered immune system and a propensity toward imbalance that can move into dis-ease. I sometimes wonder what it is that we are trying to avoid with all these practices of non-movement. This is an area for Americans to become conscious of.

I do recognize that many people work hard to get their exercise in regularly. My purpose here is to note some of the changes in our lifestyle that have made it more difficult to have a healthy amount of movement. Moving our bodies is necessary for our bones, muscles, tendons, ligaments, etc. to remain healthy, as they receive oxygen and nutrients through our movement and become stronger as a result of the movement itself.

Time

Now let's look at time, a lost commodity in our American life. We have overscheduled ourselves silly. Sometimes it is for many honorable and realistic reasons, and other times it is due to our lack of consciousness around choosing values with which we want to be aligned. We run from here to there, working most of the day; we may spend a little time with our children, put them to bed, and finish our chores, or start new projects. How much time do you spend reading a book, talking to a loved one, relaxing, noticing who you are and what you want in this life, and what you have to give? This is a HUGE problem for many of us, and it deeply affects our ability to choose health.

Questions regarding how you use your free time

1) How much free time do you have for yourself in a week?
2) How do you spend it and are you really using that free time the way you most want to?
3) What are you longing to get to that you just haven't gotten to yet?
4) Do you think you ever will get to it if you continue practicing your current lifestyle?
5) What would you have to give up to do this other thing instead?
6) Would it be an improvement on what you're doing now?
7) Could you allow yourself to do what you love?
8) What is stopping you from doing what you love?
9) Who told you that you couldn't do it?
10) What belief could you change to allow yourself to indulge in what feeds your soul?
11) Can you relax? And how does that look for you?

Following Your Passion

Our health is blocked when we are not making a contribution to the world that means something to us. Many of us don't know what we really want to do for our life's work, and many of us just aren't doing it even though we have ideas of what it would be. This not knowing and longing wears on us, spiritually at first, but then it can deepen into some major problems if it has gone on long enough. We are more susceptible to illness when we are not happy, when we are stressed and unfulfilled. Emotionally, we become more likely to go into depression, anger, mistreatment of others or bad relationships if our true self is not allowed to be expressed. This can show up in so many ways and contributes to the crazy behaviors we exhibit or read about in the paper. It is not the happy, fulfilled person who goes out to commit a violent act. Sometimes these two things don't get connected, but in a conscious world they are very connected and they have a causal relationship. Parker Palmer writes that "Violence is what happens when we don't know what to do with our suffering."

If you are wondering what your life's purpose is there are many resources for you to look into it. We need to know this because we need to feel like we bring something important into our family, community, city, or the world. Human beings long for love and acceptance from others and from ourselves, and this is what we receive when we are able to do the work we love. This is what feeds our soul, and it doesn't feel like work when it is truly right for you. Not everyone will be able to reach this goal, but having the awareness that it is possible if you really want to get there is all the support that some people will need to make it happen.

Questions to help you discern how fulfilled you are with your work or hobbies

1) Do you like your work, love your work, or wish you didn't have to do it?

2) Is your work exactly what you would like to be doing?

3) Are you fulfilled by how you spend your time each day?

4) Is there something you would prefer doing to make a living?

5) What keeps you from checking into this other thing?

6) Are you afraid?

7) Do you need support and do you know someone who could possibly give that to you?

8) Do you know what makes you feel happy, energized and fulfilled?

9) Can you find a creative way to make that your life's work?

10) Does your work give you pleasure?

11) Does your work give you what you need?

12) If you can't use your gifts, skills and passions in your work, could you find another place to bring them into your free time to fulfill yourself?

For some people, it is not realistic to leave a job at this time to follow a passion. If that is the case, it is still important to know what really energizes you and fulfills you. Even if it is not in your paid work, you can still find ways to express your passions in your hobbies or other activities in your life. It is important to feed yourself in these ways, as it affects all of your being. Your health will respond positively if you can bring the things you love into your life daily, weekly or more regularly.

Chapter 5

Solutions for a Healthier Lifestyle:
Nutrition, Diet and Consciousness Around Food

Now that we have discussed some areas of our American culture that have led to some less than healthy practices, we will move on to solutions to living a healthier lifestyle. We will start by addressing two of the topics in the last section and then move on to some new areas that will be useful to explore. These areas tend to get overlooked by many of us, but definitely affect our physical and mental health.

Nutrition and Diet

I know this can be a difficult topic for some people, so I ask you to hang in there with me and do your best to stay present as you are reading this. Our culture has shamed people for being overweight, and has been very cruel to those with weight issues. If you are one of those people who has experienced pain from this, I am sorry that has happened. I do believe that it is possible to heal from that pain and to create new habits that will help you feel better soon.

Of course we have all heard that nutrition is a basic ingredient for good health. What we eat affects how we make cells and the health of each cell. As you've heard before, we are what we eat. This is literal, and what we eat affects everything about us including our moods, our physical, energetic, emotional, and spiritual nature. What we eat and drink are the building blocks that form the foundations of our entire existence as a being of mind, body and spirit. If we overlook the importance of the food that we eat and all that we consume, we are offending the very nature of ourselves. So it would help us immensely to be conscious about what we eat and to realize the connection between the foods we eat and the way we feel in our bodies and with everything else about us.

When building a house we need to start with a good, solid foundation. We also need to do that for our bodies and the best way to do that is to eat healthy foods to achieve optimum functioning. If children learn to eat healthy food from a young age they will find healthy eating to be the norm. Even if later on they are exposed to less healthy foods, it will be easier to get them to eat a healthier diet regularly if that is what they are used to. If children eat fast food, junk food and sugar from a young age, they will learn to like that too. But doing so will adversely affect them in every way, and ultimately bring about more obvious health issues. These include increased colds and flu, ear infections (due to a lessened immune response), and even diabetes which is getting out of control for children and is in many cases due to their diet. Improper nutrition also affects children's ability to concentrate in school, can be a factor in ADD or ADHD and affects their brain growth. Eating healthy food gives children (and adults) a strong foundation to have a healthy body, mind and spirit for the rest of their lives.

Unhealthy eating habits may be caused by a lack of education around nutrition or by the seeming inability to pay for healthier food, by the lack of transportation to purchase healthy foods, or maybe parents are struggling to change their own bad habits. But let us realize the positive effects of good nutrition and really take that information in. For many people in our culture today it feels like there is an immediate shut off switch when they hear that good nutrition brings them good health. The reaction for some people is as if someone attacked them, and they psychologically go into modes of shame, defense or denial. We need to be conscious of this reaction in ourselves and work through it because I believe it is the reason some people continue to eat what they know is not healthy for them. We are a country of unconscious eaters and it is not helping our health as a whole. Our medical providers do not address this strongly enough and the state of our country's health blatantly shows us that the direction we have moved in over the last fifty years is NOT supporting basic health. Many forms of dis-ease have increased dramatically like obesity, cancer, and diabetes and I don't believe that this is randomly caused.

We need to re-learn what the foundations are for good nutrition and feed ourselves those foods that enhance our life force instead of eating things that actually take away from our life force. (See the list on page 46.) Several times a day we decide what food and drink we put into our bodies. If we were to become more educated and conscious about the effects these choices have, we would probably end up choosing healthier foods and drinks more often.

In the international best-selling book *Anti-Cancer – A New Way of Life*, David Servan-Schreiber, MD, PhD tells us about some of the reasons why changes in our lifestyle and environment have contributed to the rise of cancer and other diseases. Two of these three major factors directly relate to diet.

1) *The addition of large quantities of highly refined sugar to our diet*

2) *Changes in methods of farming and raising animals and, as a result, in our food*

3) *Exposure to a large number of chemical products that didn't exist before 1940*

Let us first look at what the large increase in consumption of sugar is doing to our bodies physiologically. Sugar, as well as white flour, have a high "glycemic index" which makes our blood glucose levels rise rapidly. Then our body releases insulin to enable the glucose to enter the cells. Along with the insulin, a molecule called IGF (insulin-like growth factor) is also secreted. IGF's role is to stimulate cell growth. What this means is that sugar feeds cancer as it promotes the factors of inflammation and stimulates cell growth which in turn act as sort of a "fertilizer" for tumors. What is really frightening to me is how dramatic the increase in sugar consumption has been over time.

In his book Dr. Servan-Schreiber explains that among people of European descent in America in 1800 a typical person ate an average of 4 lbs. of **refined sugar** in a year. In 1855 that number was 20 lbs. per year, in 1935 it was 94 lbs., and in **2000** it was **150 lbs. per year, per person**!! Wow! Another source cited that in **2009** more than 50% of Americans consumed ½ pound of sugar per day or **180 lbs. per year.** This is a phenomenal increase in sugar consumption.

He believes that the genes in our bodies have not been able to adapt to the differences in our diet that we have made in modern times as compared to when we were hunters and gatherers. We used to eat a lot of vegetables and fruit and occasionally meat or egg proteins. We are eating a different diet now. A quote from Dr. Servan-Schreiber explains:

"Western surveys of nutrition reveal that 56% of our calories today come from three sources that were nonexistent when our genes were developing.

1) Refined sugars (cane and beet sugar, corn syrup, etc.)

2) Bleached flour (white bread, white pasta, etc.)

3) Vegetable oils (soybean, sunflower, corn, trans fats)

It so happens these three sources contain none of the proteins, vitamins, minerals or omega-3 fatty acids needed to keep our bodies functioning. On the other hand, they *directly* fuel the growth of cancer."

So as it turns out, many of us are feeding our bodies foods that we were not meant to eat. No wonder we don't feel good. The *Anti-Cancer - A New Way of Life* book is filled with information that is scientifically grounded and is easy to understand. Dr. Servan-Schreiber himself is a researcher and doctor who found out he had brain cancer (twice), and then became interested in learning what he could do to keep it from coming back. The book is an amazing reference for learning to eat healthier and live longer without illness, cancer in particular. He has a whole section that is an Anti-Cancer Action Plan with tables of information that spell out what you can do to prevent cancer. He includes not only diet in his book, but also how exercising your body and working with your mind and psyche can strengthen your immune system against cancer and other diseases.

Addressing the third change in our nutritional content (and the difference in farming methods since the 1950's), Dr. Servan-Schreiber goes on to say that our physiological balance depends very much on the balance between omega-3 and omega-6 fatty acids in our body. Because we cannot make these fatty acids in our bodies we must receive them from the food we eat. So the balance of our omega-3 and omega-6 is dependent on what the animals we are eating have consumed. Unfortunately changes in our farming methods in the last fifty years led to our livestock no longer eating grass, and instead being fed corn, soy and wheat. This has resulted in a dietary imbalance in the ratio of essential fatty acids leading to the incredible overconsumption of omega-6s because the grains are full of them and are lacking omega-3s. Grass fed animals provide us with a perfect balance of these two fatty acids (a balance close to 1/1). On the other hand, animals that eat corn and soy give us imbalances in our bodies as much as 1/15 or even 1/40. The omega-3 and omega-6 present in our bodies constantly compete to control our body functions. Omega-6's help stock fats and promote rigidity in cells as well as coagulation and inflammation in response to outside aggression. Omega-3's are involved in developing the nervous system, making cell membranes more flexible, and reducing inflammation and production of adipose cells. This imbalance is precisely the factor associated with certain cancers and is also a major cause for obesity, both of which have become epidemic in the last fifty years.

This is obviously a big problem, as most of our population consumes meat, eggs and milk that come from large factory farms and this is supplying too much omega-6 to us because that's what the animals are getting from their own diet. In contrast, organically farmed, grass-fed animals supply us with balanced fatty acids and food that is not sprayed with pesticides or other chemicals. Neither are they given antibiotics or hormones like estradiol and zeranol to fatten them up faster like most factory farm animals are. Because of the importance of the omega-3 fatty acids, if you are unable to eat grass-fed meat, it is necessary to take omega-3 supplements so this nutrient is not left out of your diet and drastically unbalanced by the omega-6's.

List of foods that make up a healthy diet

1) Eat proteins from vegetables as well as from organic, grass fed or free range livestock, fish and eggs, as much as possible. If you eat meat that is not labeled in this way, you will be ingesting antibiotics, hormones and chemicals that are fed to the animals

that you eat, all of which have a negative effect on your body. You will also miss out on the necessary Omega-3's. Learn what are healthy sources of fat.

2) Eat lots of vegetables and fruits, and the more organic food you eat the better. If you cannot eat all organic fresh produce, I have included a list below that tells you the most and least contaminated produce so that you can at least buy organic to avoid the really contaminated foods.

3) Eat whole grains such as rice, oats, quinoa, millet, barley, etc. and whole grain bread as opposed to white flour products. The more milled (fine) the flour, the more it spikes your blood sugar.

4) Lower your consumption of foods with hydrogenated (trans) fats, as well as foods high in cholesterol, salt, and dairy. Eat as little processed sugar as possible. You will still get sugar in fruits and fruit juices, and these are much healthier snacks than those with processed sugar (which often contain many chemicals too). It can be surprising how many foods have natural sugar like raisins, dates, dried fruits, fresh fruits, carrots, beets, etc. Be creative and look for the above mentioned "sweet" items for new desserts or snack options that aren't full of the things that bring your life force down.

5) Keep your consumption of caffeine, soda, "energy drinks" reasonably low as they are stimulants that we can get addicted to, as well as chocolate. My guess is that many of us use them to avoid getting as much sleep as our body really needs so that we can get more and more done – ask yourself why you drink them. Soda pop has high sugar content and when it is not caffeinated or is diet pop the sweeteners used

have cancer causing ingredients. Soda pop may be a leading cause of the staggering numbers of diabetics in our country.

6) Eat a large variety of foods in a week, as opposed to always having the same foods all the time. Different vegetables, for example, will provide you with a variety of nutrients, all of which your body needs. Also it is helpful to eat foods that are in season where you live.

7) Drink lots of water, every day. There are many variables in determining how much water you need per day. It depends on the other things you put in your body, like in the case of coffee, pop or alcohol you would need even more water to replenish your cells so they are not dehydrated. It also depends on the content of water that you take in from the foods you eat. There is not one clear formula to give you – but for most people, more than what you're doing now is better. And sipping throughout the day hydrates better than the camel approach (taking in huge amounts of water a few times per day). Not to be crude, but if your urine is dark, you really need water.

If we were to cut out most of the beverages we drink other than water, this would greatly impact our caloric intake, and the health of our bodies. There are large amounts of sugar, corn syrup and chemicals in most of the beverages on the market. If you can instead drink clean, filtered tap water through carbon filter or reverse osmosis, you will get used to the flavor and you could even add some mint, thyme, sage or lemon to your water, or drink non-sugared sparkling water. Be careful of PVC's in all of the plastic containers that hold beverages, especially if they have been in the sun. Add minerals to your diet if using filtered water.

8) As a general rule, Americans eat way too much meat, sugar and other carbohydrates, and we don't eat enough vegetables. According to Servan-Schreiber, the Mediterranean, Indian and Asian cuisine is much better for us. The typical American or Western diet is literally killing us. The rate of disease, particularly cancer, is lower in Mediterranean, Indian and Asian cultures. (If you're interested in learning more about this research, please go to the book *Anti-Cancer – A New Way of Life* by David Servan-Schreiber.)

List of the Most and Least Contaminated Fruits and Vegetables 2012
(contaminated with pesticides and other chemicals)
(Source: The Environmental Working Group, www.foodnews.org)

Most Contaminated (Buying organic is preferred if at all possible)
apples, peaches, nectarines, blueberries (domestic), strawberries, grapes
also peppers, celery, potatoes, spinach, lettuce, cucumbers
+green beans and kale/greens may contain pesticide residues of special concern

Least Contaminated (Clean 15 - Lowest in pesticides)
pineapple, mango, kiwi, cantaloupe (domestic), grapefruit, watermelon
also onions, sweet corn, avocado, cabbage, sweet peas, asparagus, eggplant, sweet potatoes, mushrooms

Note: Eating conventionally grown is far better than not eating fruits and vegetables at all.

Because of my own personal sensitivity to foods, chemicals, energies, electro-magnetic fields, etc. it has been easier for me to eat and live healthier than some people because I get immediate feedback when my body says "no" to something. My son and I act as the "canary" in the coalmine for people around us. When Eli was about three years old, if he ate a grape that was not organic, he would have trouble breathing and have to be given albuterol (a drug) to help open his airways. He has had asthma that is caused by allergens, though it has greatly improved with age and his mother's healing tricks and is mostly gone now. I was not that surprised by his strong reaction, knowing my own constitution, and having read that there are forty-three pesticides on grapes that are not organically grown. He and I can feel things that others' may not feel, but that doesn't mean it isn't detrimental to the rest of the population. It's something to think about.

This is a 2005 quote from David Servan-Schreiber's book:

"In the United States, researchers at the Center for Disease Control have identified the presence of 148 toxic chemicals in the blood and urine of Americans of all ages." And "In addition to the huge increase in sugar consumption and the deterioration of the omega-6/omega-3 ratio, there has been a huge increase in toxic substances in our environment and our bodies since the Second World War. The annual production of synthetic chemicals has risen from a million tons in 1930 to two hundred million tons in 1977."

(I can only imagine how high that number is now in 2013.)

General questions to learn more about your own eating habits

1) Do you feel that you presently have healthy eating habits?

2) If not, are you in need of a little change, moderate, or big change?

3) Is this a change you think could help you feel better?

4) Did you find the above lists helpful for learning how to eat healthier?

5) Would you prefer to have a home-cooked meal or prepared food that you heat?

6) Do you have basic cooking skills or could you learn them?

7) Do you tend to eat when you are not particularly hungry?

8) Do you tend to go for long periods of time being hungry without eating?

9) How often do you eat foods that you know are not the best for you but you just can't seem to stop yourself?

10) Do you eat because you're lonely or upset?

11) Do you NOT eat because you're lonely or upset?

12) Do you think you would have a more healthy relationship with food if you were more conscious of how and what you eat?

13) Does food somehow fill the void that love of self or love of others would fill?

Being Conscious With Your Eating

One of the major ways we disconnect from our body is to eat without conscious awareness. That is in part exhibited by *what* we eat, but it also has to do with *how* we eat. Many of us eat when we are not hungry. And some of us don't eat when we are hungry. This may go back to our lack of awareness of our physical body, and to a real split, in some cases, from our body. Or it may be that we specifically lose our conscious ability to be in the moment during times of choosing and eating food.

When we eat food that we know is not healthy for us, and we're trying to eat healthy, there is a split in our intention. In the moment of choosing the food and eating it some people become fixated on the desire for that food, and forget about its undesirable aspects or future consequences. For some people this is a constant issue, and it would help to focus on bringing more conscious awareness to their eating habits, for example, by keeping a daily food log. I understand that many of us have created some less-than-healthy eating habits, (and those habits are usually unconscious), but I also want to say that it is possible to change them, and allow new, conscious habits to begin to take their place. Thinking through your food choices with conscious awareness before you eat will bring a more positive feeling to the process of eating. Once you get used to having foods around that you really would rather be eating, it can become automatic just like any other habit. You learn to say "no" to the stuff that makes you feel bad either in your body or your mind when you're preparing to eat it (or after you've eaten it). That kind of awareness is what is necessary for changing your less-than-desirable habits. This won't always be as hard as it is at the beginning of the change. To become conscious around this, ask yourself some possibly painful questions. If you have to, put notes up on your refrigerator or cupboards to remind yourself of your true intention for your nutritional desires, until you feel comfortable making decisions for yourself.

Your Food Choices - The Hard Questions

1) Am I choosing healthy food when I'm shopping for food?

2) If I'm trying to eat healthy, do I really want to buy these cookies and pastries?

3) Do I really want to put foods in my cupboards that contain a lot of calories, sugar and chemicals?

4) When I look into my shopping cart, am I happy with what I am about to bring home?

5) Do I have more vegetables, fruits, meats and whole grains than I do carbohydrates with white flour and sugar?

6) Can I put back on the shelves two things that I really want but know I'd be better off not having?

7) Can I find some healthier snack foods or desserts than those I usually eat?

8) I'm halfway through this milk shake, and I realize it is not making me feel good. Can I throw it away and remember this for the next time I think I want a milkshake?

9) What can I replace soda with so I can eliminate it from my diet? (This is one of the worst things a person can imbibe - eliminating it altogether will strengthen your body!)

10) Do I really want to stop at this fast food place and take in all that fat, sugar, calories, and chemicals instead of waiting a little longer and going home to cook, or stopping elsewhere for a healthier bite to eat?

It is important to remember that the advertisements we see everywhere are there for someone else to profit from monetarily. YOU are the one who chooses if you want to support those companies that make foods and drinks that are blatantly unhealthy. These companies will be around as long as people buy from them. You are voting every day for their existence or their downfall. Our country's health will not improve if we keep doing what we have been doing. Take it to heart. You are worth it.

For Those Who Under-Eat

When we are hungry but don't feel we have time to eat, this is also a real problem. Sometimes we don't eat because of our stress levels. I will talk more about this in the next chapter. Unfortunately not eating can mess up our blood sugar levels and deplete us in many ways. This can keep us from accomplishing the very task that we thought we had to get done before we could take the time to eat. Having nutritional snacks available in those moments are a quick and easy way to help one hang in there until a full meal is available. I usually carry some almonds or a protein bar with me in my purse because my blood sugar levels can cause me to feel spacey or not altogether myself if I'm in need of food. Once you become used to taking care of yourself in this way it is quite simple. What it requires is checking in with your body more often and thinking ahead so you can answer the need for nutrition quickly.

If you are the person who is prone to under-eating or being too busy to eat, please start your day with a healthy breakfast high in protein. (This is really good for anyone.) Next it would be important for you to learn to listen to your body and actually stop what you're doing to ask the question, "Do I need some nutrition (food) right now?" Once you take your attention off of what you were doing and check in with your body you might notice feeling tired or weak, brain fog or even hungry. Then you can stop and give yourself some healthy food instead of stressing your body trying to stretch its capacity on little or no nutrition. It is not helpful to do this. The drop in blood sugar for some people can be very disruptive to their system. Sometimes the body then has to tap into using the adrenal glands for instance, which are meant to be used for fight or flight, and not for general overwork. Many of us are too intense about getting things done, and our bodies pay the price for this. American culture leans this way to keep us going, and we rely on caffeine and sugar and "energy drinks," which can lead to adrenal burnout. I can tell from my energy work with clients that most Americans are overusing their adrenal glands for pushing through all that they feel they need to get done. I put myself in that category as well and empathize with the dilemma. At least I am conscious of it so there is opportunity for change.

Emotional Eating

When the answer to the question "am I hungry?" is "no" but you eat anyway, this is called emotional eating, and it is done unconsciously, at least for a while. I believe that in this case there is usually some need that is not being met, so a person uses food to meet that need instead of discerning what else might be more appropriate for the situation. It becomes much easier to give ourselves food than to go into some deeper pain. There are many people who eat because they feel stressed, afraid, anxious, ashamed, unlovable or a variety of other difficult emotions, and temporarily it makes them feel better. But this behavior further disconnects people from their body, mind and spirit. It can become very painful the longer it goes on, and it often becomes habitual. If this sounds like your situation, I strongly recommend getting some help from a professional. I am not an expert on this, but Geneen Roth, a New York Times best-selling author has written many books on the subject. Some of her books include *Feeding the Hungry Heart, Breaking Free from Emotional Eating, When Food is Love and Women, Food and God*. There are also specific therapists for eating disorders if you feel you need help. In general, all psychotherapists are trained to help you with unprocessed emotions that may be causing you to overeat.

Another way people overeat is just by eating too much at one time. Some people do not pay attention to when they are full, and they eat way more than is necessary or helpful. Eating too much food puts a strain on your digestive system. Our body spends a tremendous amount of energy every day digesting food. If we overeat, the energy will be used for digesting because that is an immediate need, and that means that other body systems will not be getting as much energy as they may need to do their work most effectively. Your lungs may not be getting enough energy to clear the mucus in them, your brain may not be thinking as clearly because so much blood is being used in the intestines, or the cut on your finger may take longer to heal. We sometimes think that no matter what we do to our body, it will just keep on pushing. And in some ways that is true. The body can and does do an infinite number of things all at once in every second of our lives. But it has a limited amount of energy to do it with. So if you eat a well-balanced diet and only as much as you need you will be assisting your body to use its life force energy in the most judicious ways possible. You may find that you have more energy to be creative, exercise or read, or spend time with friends if you can stop over-eating.

I have an interesting story about this very thing. I am typically very good at not over-eating, but I have recognized something about over-eating that I want to share with you. When I was on a cruise (the best place in the world to overeat) I noticed how hungry I became between meals. On the cruise I was eating much more, and doing much less activity than I usually do in my regular life. There was no way I could reconcile this, other than to think that by over-eating I was stretching out my stomach beyond its usual size or boundaries, making it able to take in more food, and wanting to take in more food. When it became empty I felt ravenous, and yet my calorie and nutrition intake was far beyond my norm. I decided that whatever signal detects my hunger had been reset at a new position, and it took place in a matter of a couple days. I asked one of my traveling companions if this was happening to her, and she said no, she had no idea of what I was talking about. She is a person who often over-eats, so it was more of a normal intake for her. I found this so interesting, and fortunately when I went home, I was able to reset my hunger "button" to the regular amount of food I typically take in, and hence drop the pounds that I had gained on the cruise.

I think it is likely that most of us eat way more than we need. Restaurants give us servings that are too big and many of us eat this same way at home as well. Becoming conscious in this area of portion control is extremely helpful to those who wish to lose or maintain their current weight.

Recognizing what is the optimal amount of food for you will make it easier to eat in healthier ways. Eating when you are hungry, and not eating just because the clock tells you its lunch time is a much more integrated approach to creating healthy eating habits. Listening to your body when it is full is also useful. Some say it takes 10-15 minutes for the stomach to signal the brain that it is full, so it's better to stop eating way before you feel "stuffed." Of course there may be an occasion like a big holiday during which you might eat more than usual. You also may notice how tired you feel after that big meal. This is a choice we all make. I have learned that if I eat only a little more than usual, I will feel much better overall than if I really overeat. It has become worth it to me to keep the food at an amount where I am still comfortable in my body. This choice has come through years of bodily awareness and knowledge about how I affect my body when I give it too much food or the wrong foods. It is just not worth it to me to do that anymore. I practice this by questioning myself in the moment about what is good for me, and what I could really do without. I am so much happier in the moment and the next day.

Pointers for Losing Weight or Maintaining Current Weight

(This is meant to be used by adults)

1) Eat three healthy, moderate meals a day, including lots of different vegetables, a protein source, and moderate amount of carbohydrates (whole grains, breads, starches), and maybe some fruit. Some people think it is better to eat fruits and vegetables separately because our body uses two opposing enzymes to help us digest each of them.

2) Avoid eating a late evening meal or later nighttime snacks. I try not to eat anything after 8:00 p.m. This allows me to burn those calories before I go to bed. If I feel hungry after 8:00p.m. I tell myself that I am burning calories and will be back to the size I like in the morning.

3) Engage in minimal or no snacking between meals, depending on your weight goals. If you choose them, have low-calorie snacks like fruit or vegetables and foods low in sugar and other carbs. Some people need snacks high in protein. When you eat sugar alone, as in cookies, etc. between meals it spikes your insulin which is not good if you're trying to lose weight or avoid getting cancer.

4) When you eat out, be aware of the volume of food you're eating (portion control), paying attention to how your stomach feels and take home your leftovers for lunch. Or split the dinner with your dining companions.

5) Part of being aware of your eating is to be fully present and conscious of what you're eating as you're

doing it. Slow yourself down and really taste each bite and savor it. This awareness can help lower your consumption if you're attempting to eat less.

6) Avoid desserts and sugar as much as possible. It takes your body five days to physiologically not crave sugar. If you can go that long, you will be craving it only with your mind (which is no small deal), but you may be surprised how the desire for it becomes a lot less strong. (Remember that sugar is food for cancer cells.) Or allow yourself reasonable-sized desserts or other sugar treats once or twice a week, or whatever goal or rule you set and then stick to it.

7) Avoid beverages other than water or tea to cut calories. Drink a lot of water. If you have tea or coffee, try to use a healthy sweetener. Certainly avoid white granulated sugar.

8) Exercise or move, move, move regularly. Make it fun!

9) Believe it or not, meditation may help you lose weight by bringing all of your body and mind's functions into perfect alignment, resonating with each other effortlessly. This can result in hormone changes and proper metabolic function, especially if the adrenal glands can calm down.

10) Try to think of food less, for example, only when it is time to shop or prepare your meals.

11) Incessant thoughts around food will make you hungrier and eat more. Your body does not need to eat all day long, and in fact, it much prefers the break from digestion.

"Those who think they have not time for bodily exercise will sooner or later have to find time for illness."
— *Edward Stanley*

Chapter 6
Solutions for a Healthier Lifestyle:
Exercise

Exercise can be another sensitive topic for some people. Again, I ask you to consciously stay with me as we explore this area, especially if you are someone who would benefit from creating new habits around movement and exercise. I understand that shame can creep in when exercise is brought up, and I suggest that you keep your head up and remember that NOW is the most important moment. THIS is the moment that you can choose to do something different if you want to. We all have our challenges in life and this may be yours. I recommend that you take in the words that you need and leave the rest.

Our bodies need exercise to be at their optimal fitness level and even just to maintain adequate health. To be strong, balanced and healthy we need vigorous exercise or movement for good cardiovascular health (30 minutes 3-5 times a week), we need to keep our muscles strong (and useful), and also to maintain flexibility (do more stretching, especially as you age). Vigorous movement oxygenates our body, bringing in both oxygen and nutrients through our blood and into all of our tissues, bones and organs to assist them in working at an optimal level. Movement helps prevent blockages, both physical and energetic, keeping the regular flow open.

Studies have shown that if you exercise you can reduce and even reverse your rate of aging. Deepak Chopra talks about this in several of his books. One study I read focused on women between 65-70 who had never exercised previously and learned to do weight training. Their bodies became stronger and they felt less pain and were able to do more things in their life than before. They also strengthened their bones, which is very helpful for aging women who become prone to osteoporosis and bone breaks after menopause. It seems that it doesn't matter when you start, exercise will always be beneficial. "Movement is improvement" is one true and short mantra. I often tell my clients, "It's either use your body or lose it." Unfortunately, that is the reality. If you stop going up and down steps or lifting something that is a bit of a challenge for you, you will no longer be able to do those things when you need to or want to.

Exercise can be one of those things that people learn to do as a young person, and if that is the case, it is usually easier to maintain when you're older, as it can become habitual. Regular exercise can become a habit for both mind and body. In either case we may feel a real need to exercise for our well-being especially if we've been doing it for years. This is a strong reason to have children run and play active games or sports when they're young, in preparation for an active exercise regimen as they age. But no matter what age, we can all learn new habits if we decide to.

Discerning your habits around exercise

1) Did you like to run and play as a kid, or play sports?

2) Do you regularly exercise now at least three times per week, or would you like to?

3) Do you enjoy exercising? This includes playing tennis, volleyball, basketball, walking, running, hiking, canoeing, biking, roller-blading or any number of other sports.

4) Do you do other things to move like vacuuming, gardening, raking, mowing or walking?

5) If you have an exercise regime, does it give you stress relief and clear your mind?

6) Can you tell that you are stronger or more energetic when you exercise or move?

7) If you don't exercise regularly, would you like that to be part of your life?

8) What would it take for you to start exercising at this time or to increase the current amount of time you spend at it?

9) Can you think of one activity that you enjoy that gets your body moving?

10) If you have resistance around exercising, can you think of where it comes from, and could you talk to someone to help you process and resolve this resistance?

11) If you knew that you could feel better and live longer with regular exercise, would it give you incentive to begin or to take your current program more seriously?

Exercising can give you a lot of satisfaction and encourage positive feelings for example, feeling strong and vital, or becoming relaxed and sleeping better. One of the areas that gets forgotten in regard to exercise is that it can be a time to experience real connection with your body in a way that is different than usual. This conscious awareness is helpful because you can learn new information about yourself that might be useful to know. For instance you might realize one day that you are very tired, or that your neck is sore, or recognize something else you had no awareness of until you tuned into your body. If you're really tired and "off" you might ask yourself why? If you know you were up too late for a couple nights in a row that is very logical. Or is it possible you're beginning to get sick? If you think that is it, you could sleep more, take some supplements to stimulate and strengthen your immune system, or you might choose to get acupuncture (to help balance your system) or take a sea salt bath (to pull out toxins). If you don't take the time to notice your body and how it is feeling you might end up sick. You may choose to look at your work out time as a gift to reconnect with your inner self, which includes your body, mind and spirit. It's a sort of check-in time because in our busy lives it is easy to lose touch with where we are physically, emotionally, mentally and spiritually. Checking in is a conscious action. You will find that every time you do this there will be different information to receive because all of these aspects are in a constant state of change.

Exercise for Body Awareness

This is most easily done in a quiet place by starting with three or more deep breaths to help you settle into yourself. You can check all three levels of your being if you wish, asking what you notice in your mind or mental state, what you notice in your body, and what you notice in your spirit. You might ask yourself if you've taken any time for self-care lately, or if you've been running from one thing to the next with no breaks. You may determine if you feel calm or anxious lately, or are you generally happy or unhappy with your life lately? By checking in with yourself, you will be more likely to make small or large changes in your behavior that could be just what you need to get yourself back in balance. This can help you have a more satisfying life experience and ultimately lead to better health.

When I am working out I have been able to notice small changes in myself because I am paying attention to my body (in particular, but I can often get a sense of the bigger picture too). I am able to recognize more strength or the ability to move in a way that used to be "stuck" with a new ease. For me, it is the healing of my old car accident wounds, like scar tissue releasing (from body work I receive or from doing yoga) or a new strength where there had once been weakness. I can still see the changes taking place twenty-five years later, which is truly exciting. Two years ago I was finally able to run in a full sprint for the first time since the accident, and it felt exhilarating. I used to be a soccer player and was the fastest one on the team. It has been sad and difficult for me to be unable to run without encountering pain. I feel younger and a sense of freedom due to this one renewed ability.

One of the laws of energy is that it moves with intention. As you are exercising, you may wish to pay close attention to see how your body is responding to the activity you're doing. This of course will be most valuable if you are present to yourself, meaning not reading or listening to music (unless you can also tune into your body at the same time you listen). These distractions are another way that we keep from observing just what is going on with our body. Instead, you could focus conscious awareness on your legs and breathe as you stretch, for example, and it is likely you will be able to take the stretch farther or deeper than the last time you did it. When you are running on the treadmill you could focus consciously on an emotion like anger that you would like to release out of your body. In fact, all exercises that use your legs like swimming, running, biking, using the elliptical machine, dancing or even stomping, help to move the energy of anger out of the body. (Speaking in energy terms it is because the first chakra is where anger gets stuck, and the first chakra connects to your hips.) So if you were to focus on *feeling* the situation and the ensuing anger, and then focus on releasing the anger intentionally as you are doing your exercise, releasing the charge of the anger is likely to happen.

Remember the idea that your body is like a river? It is so true, and you will notice this if you pay attention to your body as you go through your workout and afterwards. For me, I become very aware of the small differences within my body even a few days after I just exercised. I can tell when I am a bit stronger, or a bit more tired, or that a muscle is contracted that usually isn't because I'm not able to stretch as far as before. Then I may ask myself, "what has changed within my life to show up in my physical body in this way?" And I also can notice my regular cycle of energy that changes throughout the month. The benefit of this is it helps me learn how to work *with* my body and not against it, respecting how it flows and changes and modify what I ask of it accordingly. Besides helping to notice and respond to my body's needs, I also notice how responsive my body really is. When I have to skip working out if I'm out of town, for instance, I am always amazed at how much I miss the workout and how quickly my body will shift away from the strength I am used to having. It doesn't take more than a week to notice the difference, and usually it takes just three or four days for me to notice that I'm not as strong or that I am feeling more tired and less alert. But when I get back into my regular routine it is easy to bring myself back to where I was, and then continue moving forward in flexibility and strength. I really appreciate how my body responds to the movement and exercise that I give it, and that helps me to know I am doing the right things for it. As an aside, the more regular your exercise becomes, the quicker you recover from the lack of exercise during times of sickness, vacation or whatever takes you away from your exercise routine.

Even in illness, we still need some exercise or movement, which may seem counterintuitive. In reality, moving your body will often help you move through an illness at a faster rate. Now I don't mean when you are having a fever or vomiting. I'm talking more about a slight imbalance like a cold or cough, or chronic illnesses such as arthritis, diabetes, heart disease, etc. I have found that if I feel a bit off balance in my health (which I tend to notice quickly), and I seem to be coming down with something, working out lightly can usually keep it from becoming an illness that would keep me away from my normal life routines. It is rare that I am down and out with an illness, partly because of this, and partly because of my general health, body awareness and knowledge around keeping myself well. It really pays off to have good body awareness if you're interested in keeping yourself from getting sick.

There are a few other things that I have found important to keep oneself on a regular exercise schedule. The first is that if it is not a priority for you it will be the first thing to go out of your weekly schedule. Make it a priority by writing it down in your calendar, on your smart phone or computer schedule and don't allow anything else to take the place of it. Exercising is a sacred time. It is one type of self-care, and when I miss it I definitely do not function at my optimum, nor am I as happy. If I don't feel exactly energetic that morning because I was up too late the night before, so be it. I go anyway. Being regular no matter how you feel is the only way to create a healthy habit of exercising. Ninety-nine percent of the time I will feel better afterward and because I know this, I will not skip unless I feel horribly sick. I exercise at my health club only twice a week, but I have done that for twenty-six years straight for two hours each time. I also get "exercise" doing my massage work three or four other days in the week, plus walking, biking, yardwork, etc.

Also, it is important to like what you are doing when you work out, so that you get the full benefit of your efforts. Many types of movement are not thought of as exercise but they really are, for instance dancing, walking in the woods, or building a deck. There are so many options these days for getting exercise, so choose something you can enjoy. If exercising is not a chore you will obviously do it more often. If you're looking for something new, you could try yoga, chi gung, tai chi, or weight lifting, kettle bells, swimming, kick-boxing, pilates or other activities or classes. There are endless options for movement or exercise and the most important thing is not what you do, but that you do something and do it regularly. And when you do, remember to notice how good you feel afterward and give yourself kudos for actually doing it!

"When we walk to the edge of all the light we have and take the step into the darkness of the unknown, we must believe one of two things will happen — there will be something solid to stand on, or we will be taught to fly."

— *Patrick Overton*

Chapter 7
Solutions for a Healthier Lifestyle:
Working with Emotions

Emotions and Health

Ever since I was a kid, I've been a highly sensitive and emotional person. Maybe because I am astrologically a Cancer... they say we're moody. Unfortunately, I didn't express my feelings as freely as I needed to as a child, so I experienced physical symptoms. I was one of those kids (and I know many of you can relate) who put all my stress in my intestinal area. (The particular place of vulnerability is not of importance; the point is that it has to go somewhere if it is not expressed.) I would have pain that would bring me to the nurse's office at school, or the pain would begin when I got home. It was many a night that I was having pain that caused me to tell my parents "I have another bellyache." My childhood was not easy, and my parents were divorced when I was 10. This was a lot for a little girl who was very sensitive to "digest." I didn't do it all that well; I had my appendix out at age 11 and was "diagnosed" with irritable bowel syndrome at age 15. In the past 20 years this has not been a major problem for me, due to my awareness that caused me to shift my behaviors and heal the underlying issue. I have had to do some very deep work to release the negative patterns I had created as a child. Even now when I become very stressed, my intestinal area may have mild symptoms that tell me I am out of balance. This is my body's wisdom coming through my vulnerable area to tell me to do something different, to respond in a loving or more positive way to my body and my life.

We all have our reasons for not expressing our emotions in a healthy way. But do you know that the lack of expression may be depleting your body's immune system? Not only can holding in our emotions become physical problems if not addressed, but often the problems that are expressed physically are specifically related to the issues we are having difficulty with in our emotional and psychological lives.

I have learned that the place where our body succumbs to dis-ease, is not purely coincidental. There is a theory of body symbology that is remarkable. It relates the part of the body that is having problems to the role or purpose that that part plays in our physiological system. For instance, it was not a coincidence that I was having problems with the digestion of my food. I was also having problems with my mental/emotional digestion of my home life, and that imbalance was not corrected in a short enough time to keep me from manifesting a physical response to my stress. My intestines acted as a messenger to me (or to my parents) that something was off, and I was unable to literally "take in the nutrients I was receiving and release the garbage" (in this case the emotional pain). This is the way body symbology works. I use the concept with my clients regularly, and it continues to amaze me how consistently the issues they are having in their lives relate to the problems they are having in their bodies. This information can help us know what direction to take to heal the emotional, mental, spiritual, or physical problem. The section on body symbology in Chapter 12 explores this idea more deeply.

Physicians trying to discern why there is imbalance (dis-ease) in the body may overlook the influence that stress, emotions and our responses to them have on physical health. Quite often our physical body is not where "dis-ease" starts. The problem often begins in a mental, spiritual or energetic part of ourselves. If that part is imbalanced for a period of time, which is variable for each person, then the body will become less able to fight the "invader" and surrender to an illness or disease. We now know that when the body/mind experiences chronic stress over a period of time, it can begin to lower our immune function. There is also a genetic component to illness, but newer research suggests that our old single-gene theory is quickly being abandoned as is the idea that our genes are fixed. We may have the gene that creates a propensity for a particular disease but it does not necessarily mean we will get that condition. According to Deepak Chopra in his book *Reinventing the Body, Resurrecting the Soul,* everyone's body is the end product of a lifelong process that turns our gene switches on or off according to our experiences. This means that we have an opportunity to turn on and off a gene that is on a fixed schedule. We also have an opportunity to turn on and off a gene depending on our behavior and experiences, or a third option is that a gene may turn on and off as a combination of the two former examples. The good news is that for the vast majority of our genes, nature and nurture play a crucial role. It appears that much of what leads us to succumbing to disease may be found in our own coping skills. What we have in our mind and emotions and thoughts contributes to our immune function, either weakening or strengthening it through the hormonal output that instigates the immune system to fight back or shut down.

Sickness and disease can come from a germ, virus or bacteria, but even then our surrender to that "bug" is likely the result of a suppressed immune system, which in turn may be due to a lack of strength and balance in the emotional, mental, or spiritual part of our being. This can be where our imbalance begins. Some of you may not agree with this, or may not know what to think about it, but for now, just think of it as one possibility. As they say in Alcoholics Anonymous, "Take what you like and leave the rest."

If you are able to wrap your mind around this theory, it puts a lot of responsibility on each individual for their own healing and health. (For many of us, that's right where we want it, instead of being at the mercy of doctors who do not know us as well as we know ourselves.) It is a lot of work to be conscious and aware of the parts of ourselves that we may not want to look at. The alternative can be feeling out of control, sick, tired and like a victim who has no power over their health issues. I want to be clear here. It is not our "fault" that we come down with illnesses. But our lack of balance in all areas of our lives, and ignoring or denying some parts of ourselves, can certainly lead to the creation of an illness. And this is a cultural problem, not only an individual issue. There is no room here for blame. We all have a belief system. We may have accepted or resisted the "system" that I call the Western medicine model. This is a system of trying to fix a condition after it becomes a major issue, instead of working with a minor one from the start to get at the origin of the problem. I know of many people who do not seek health care until they are in crisis. We have healthcare problems in this country partly because we aren't conscious of imbalance early enough to shift our thinking or behavior before we have a serious problem. We also haven't put nearly enough resources into wellness and prevention. This is costing us all a lot of pain, money, and time. It is now affecting our country so greatly that we are in the midst of a big debate over how we can continue with the costs of our present health care system.

But let us get back to emotions. The problem again lies in our American culture. We have been taught to "be nice" at all cost. Usually the greatest cost of this is our own health. We have not been taught how to deal with negative emotions, which we all have since we are human beings. There are appropriate ways to deal with our negative emotions, but instead of teaching our children these, we have managed to teach them to be good, to not rock the boat, to not say anything that displeases us, and in so doing, to ignore whatever they feel. This is why some people will not express emotions they deem as "bad," even to themselves. They get their emotions mixed up with who they are. **WE ARE NOT OUR EMOTIONS, WE HAVE EMOTIONS.** We also have the power to not let them HAVE us. If we were to allow them to move through us without judging them as being good or bad, they would just continue to flow, and we would move on to the next thing in life. Look at a young child who will be angry at their friend one minute, and over it in the next minute calling them their best friend. This is a healthy release of emotion, with no attachment to it. When we try to stop our negative emotions, they fester inside and get bigger and more destructive, because to our energy body they are a blockage. After we suppress them long enough they can become arthritis, heart disease, cancer, depression or anything else our body is vulnerable to.

There are two excellent books on this topic: *Heal Your Body and You Can Heal Your Life* by Louise L. Hay. Hay explains how mental causes can bring on physical illnesses, and gives affirmations designed to create healing in yourself. I have used these as resources throughout the many years of my practice and at least 95% of the time the client expresses that yes, in fact, the stated probable cause for the illness is true for them. Many psychotherapists and healers have written about their experiences with clients that have led them to believe that the underlying basis of most health problems would be solved if we all deeply loved and accepted ourselves. This is something to think about.

Questions to help you learn more about your relationship with your emotions

1) Are you a person who keeps your emotional life well hidden from others?

2) Can you express a difficult emotion to someone you really care about?

3) When someone asks you how you are, can you be honest with them?

4) Are you able to let someone know when you feel sad and ask for support or cry with them?

5) Are you afraid of your anger or grief?

6) Can you be upset about something and still love yourself at the same time?

7) Can you deal with conflict well when it comes up in your relationships?

8) Do you typically know how you're feeling throughout the day?

9) Would you like to learn healthier ways to deal with your feelings?

10) Have you ever journaled about your feelings or gone to a counselor/therapist?

Our culture doesn't tend to express emotions easily or well, whether they are negative or positive emotions. It is also true that many of us don't have much awareness of our emotional selves. Just like some of us don't know how our bodies feel, some also don't know what emotional state we're in. This comes from this whole realm of life being ignored; one might say we have become numb or partially numb. My belief is that this has happened due to fear, shame and possibly from feeling overwhelmed. We fear we won't be received correctly; we fear our spouse will not love us if we express anger; we fear we are not good enough and therefore must act really good to be worthy of love and acceptance. All of these fears keep us from being authentic in the world. Yet every one of us has negative emotions as well as positive ones.

Let's go to the positive emotions for a minute. If we were able to express our enthusiasm, our love, our joy, or our support more easily to those people around us, would it then be easier to express our grief, our pain, our anxiety or our anger as well? I think it would be. It seems to me we have become fairly frozen on both sides of the equation. All of this frozen, held-in emotion is so hard on our nervous systems, our bodies, our minds, our entire being. Our health needs us to JUST HAVE OUR FEELINGS!! This doesn't mean rampant wild behavior. It doesn't mean irresponsible expression. We are more likely to go in that direction though the longer we have held in our feelings.

People who fear their feelings are usually acting on an old belief that was put in place when they were young. It could be that it was scary to express negative emotions for reasons such as rejection, anger or shame directed back at them, or because they were afraid they may do something they would later regret. It is not anger itself that is dark. It is what you might do with it that could be dark or unacceptable. But if you were aware enough to know what is going on inside of you, you could choose to release or express your anger in any number of acceptable ways. I will go into some of these outlets later in the chapter.

Grief is another emotion our culture struggles to express, so we may keep it inside and it grows. Many of us hold onto grief over and over again until one accident or illness or death finally pushes us over the edge, and it becomes too big in us to keep it in any longer, and we may go into a time of grief that seems to last forever. When a loved one dies, it is imperative that we allow ourselves the time it takes to release the grief from our bodies. And this grief will come and go for some time because it is a cyclical emotion, meaning we can't remove it or go through it all at once. It takes time and energy, love and acceptance of "what is" for grief to heal enough for us to move on. We may never completely get past the feeling of loss of that person, yet we can move on in our life and use the strength of our love for them and their love for us to continue our life's work. Longstanding grief, as we all have heard, can literally break the heart of a loved one. It can also help a person create something they may have never dreamed possible, like a foundation in someone's honor, a work of art, or a new cause to bring awareness to an illness. That is the beauty of awareness and choice - consciousness.

Our emotional state is healthiest if we allow our emotions to flow through us, without attaching too much to them, but noticing them and using them as information to redirect ourselves if necessary. If we were to stay current with our flowing emotional states, we would accept them as parts of us that move and change, and they would give us pertinent information about ourselves and what is going on around us. Also, if we were mindful with our emotions they would not have the negative charge that many of them carry due to stuffing and building them up inside ourselves, then adding a little resentment, and topping that off with the self-judgement that we shouldn't be feeling that way anyhow. What if we could trust ourselves to be real and to show others who we are? We don't trust ourselves because of fear of rejection, or lack of self-esteem, or maybe it's not socially acceptable depending on the situation or our relationship with those around us. These are unconscious choices that we make on a regular basis. Because they are unconscious we often react to others in situations (instead of choosing our behavior) and we fear our own reactions because they are not choices that we have made in our conscious mind. This can make us feel out of control.

There was a time in my life, about two years after my car accident that I realized, while receiving a massage, that the emotion I was experiencing at that moment was current pain. It was no longer the deep and complex pain of my childhood, it was a lighter cry that had to do with something occurring right then in my life. I had cried and cried so many tears and processed so many emotions and thoughts and beliefs for those two years, and in that moment I knew I was finally caught up from my past and was operating in present time. I then felt extreme gratitude for my hard work and love of self that had brought me through those really difficult years. It was also then that I decided to become a massage therapist and healer, so that I could help guide others through their own healing journeys, hoping others would recognize the rewards of their efforts.

What Then, Do We Do With Emotions?

Let us look at the emotions that come and go through us daily. Let's say you're at work and someone does something that really makes you feel mad, for example, you overhear someone saying negative words about your project. If you could register that emotion of anger in your conscious awareness that would be the first step. For most people that in itself would be an improvement on what they usually do. Unfortunately we usually react internally or verbally either at the "offending person" or quite often direct a negative reaction toward ourselves. (In psychology, this is called the mask self.) We leave behind the original emotion of anger (in this case) and instead remember the parental voices *"you've messed up again"* that have kept us in line and told us how to behave so that we will be loved and accepted. Once we hear those voices we immediately berate ourselves for even having this negative emotion, and now it becomes a negative thought and emotion turned inward. Energetically we have become completely stuck, and energy that doesn't move will create something we don't want, possibly depression, possibly illness, but certainly something because it has to go somewhere.

So first, become aware of your emotion, taking note of the original emotion before all of the above happens. Then own it, by saying to yourself "I am angry at_____ because…" It is your emotion, which means it is has gone through the lens of all your experiences and all of the things that have shaped you to be the person that you are today. You have every right to have this emotion, and it is not up for debate. That is true and yet, you may choose to feel it internally and notice why you are having this emotion around this circumstance that just took place. Sometimes all we need to do is FEEL the emotion which means to ALLOW it to be there, noticing it, acknowledging its presence, and not judging it. It just is. In many cases, that is all it takes to move it through the body and the energy system and out.

If not, you may go into further analysis to shed some light on what you just experienced. For example, you may internally ask yourself if there is a part of the person's opinion that is true or useful for you to realize. Remember it was your experience, not necessarily that anyone else did anything wrong. Nor did you necessarily do anything wrong, but certainly you were triggered or you would not have felt angry. What was the trigger? Was it the one that says, "I'm not good enough," or "I have to be perfect," or "They are so stupid?" These beliefs carry our own wounds to be reconciled and other people's words and actions will likely bring them to the surface so that we can face and conquer them. Because these beliefs are usually unconscious, slowing down enough to allow them to come to the surface and into conscious awareness will bring something new to our perceptions of the interaction. These perceptions can also bring new healing of the old beliefs.

Then we can go a step further as we bring in personal responsibility for our feelings *and* compassion for ourselves for being imperfect, as we all are. Although we don't want to admit that, the truth of being human is that we are all imperfect. Not only are we imperfect, we all have our wounds (not just some of us). Because of that reality, it is extremely important that we learn to love ourselves in our imperfect state, in our true duality of being human. If we can accept our own limitations and imperfections, we will be better able to allow our feelings to flow through us, and it will become easier to accept and have compassion for the limitations and imperfections in others as well.

Releasing Old Deeply Held Emotions

When you decide to reconcile yourself and clear up your long squelched emotions so as to become current with them you will need a lot of love, patience and self-acceptance. We are all doing the best we can with something that is not easy. This is a healing journey that may be the most life-changing and life-giving project you've ever taken on. Usually a person decides it is time for this to happen when they have hit some sort of bottom in their life or when some larger experience brings them to a realization that they simply MUST change. It may be an illness, accident or some other major loss or event in their life; but whatever it is, it becomes blatantly apparent that things are no longer working, and it is time to face the hard stuff. This experience will probably go to the core of your being. Thankfully, when you begin to see healthier ways of being from a new perspective, with less fear and more conscious awareness, love and connection, you will see the rewards of your hard work. It is worth doing even if a person is not in a difficult place in life, but most of us will not go there until we must.

Doing this work requires a deep surrender into all that has been, an acceptance that what has happened in your life is in the past, and it was what it was. It is not WHO you are though, it was just your experience, and yes, it did shape you. Just support the work you are now doing, and know that it is an act of love not only for yourself, but for the larger community.

Getting started on releasing old, held emotions:
- Feel everything you have not allowed yourself to feel before.
- You may need to stomp, scream, yell, cry, wail, or whatever it takes to feel and release, feel and release.
- It might be helpful to write about it as you feel your emotions, journaling can also be cathartic.
- You may need to move your body to assist with the releasing.

- Definitely give yourself breaks from this work and get extra sleep – it can be exhausting.

This is a process, and the time it will take you is as long as it takes. You will only know how long it will be when it is done, or when you feel freedom and a shift (or many shifts) in yourself. One might say it is never done, but I don't really believe that. It is possible to become current with your emotions and then from there you will need to continue processing them as they come along again. The good news is it's possible they will not be as strong or intense in the same way as they were before your hard work. They will be much more easily felt, expressed and dealt with, and much more quickly. If you were to stop processing them regularly, it is possible your emotions would become backed up again. Hopefully your habits will change enough with the work you've done to not have this happen. Staying current is the best remedy.

Because this work can be very intense, it may best be done with another person's help, for example, a psychotherapist, massage therapist or other body-worker, but it doesn't have to be. Especially if you are a person who wants to do it alone, please be open to getting some support from someone in your life as you move through it. There is also a lot you could process if you followed some of the many books written on this topic of self-healing. One of the best I've encountered is Barbara Ann Brennan's book *Light Emerging: A Journey of Personal Healing.* This is an incredibly well-written book that includes exercises to raise your consciousness and process matters of mind, body and spirit. There may come a point in your journey where you get a little stuck on your own and you need a therapist, a healer or a loved one to help you process as you move through and beyond a difficult place. It is important at some point to feel validated for all you have gone through and all you have suffered, which requires another person to be a loving witness. I have found this to be true through my experiences with helping others heal, and I strongly recommend that this be included in your healing.

Going through years of hanging onto anger, grief, anxiety or fear is not a tea party. As you experience this old pain, it will at some point become exhausting. Keep pushing through it, as unfortunately there is no way to go around it, only through it. There will be relief and a lighter sense of being with each catharsis. Give yourself LOTS of self-care during this time. You will need more sleep, and maybe much more, because emotional exhaustion requires it. Be as loving as you can be to yourself. Remember to give yourself the kindness and compassion that you would give to your best friend if he or she was doing something similar. We are too hard on ourselves in general. This can be the opportunity that allows you to shift that way of being forever. You are a beautiful person who deserves peace, happiness, purpose and love of self to be in your life. This new way of relating to yourself and the world around you will bring you much more energy and will allow you to more easily do the real work you came here to do.

Other Ideas for Processing Emotions

1) Movement will help bring emotion through us more quickly. Exercising regularly helps maintain a healthy emotional state as it provides a release. Anytime you feel blocked up with emotion or stress, go take a walk, or move your body in some way to literally help move the energy out. If you focus on anger, for instance, while you use the elliptical machine or go running, with the intention of letting it come out of your body with each step, the emotion will usually move out quickly. One spiritual law is that "Energy moves with intention." It works well here.

2) When you can't immediately process an emotion that seems important to you - because you're at work, or with your kids, or for whatever reason, tell yourself you will get back to it later. Then give yourself 10 or

20 minutes later that day or as soon as possible, to go back to that moment and see what happened inside of you. This is how we gain insights about ourselves so that we can grow and feel more confident in a similar situation the next time it comes up.

3) Set an amount of time that you give to yourself to release emotions (this would likely be alone) and be crabby, complaining, crying, angry or anything else. After this time you may wish to journal or rest or do something that you really enjoy.

4) For grief you may find it useful to watch a sad movie or one that really pulls on your heartstrings. It will assist you in releasing your grief. In my experience I start crying over the movie and then that goes into a deeper grief of my own that needs to be released.

5) When in conflict with another person you may wish to express your feelings by taking turns expressing "my reality" to the other person for a timed period. During that time the other person only listens with no comments or advice. Then you switch partners. This helps us feel validated or better understood by those we are in relationship with.

6) When releasing emotions in the presence of others, be conscious of not splattering them energetically *at* people. This simply means expressing your emotions out and away from a person's body as opposed to into someone's body. You will appreciate this in return.

7) Also when you're working with others, take responsibility for your emotions instead of blaming others for how you feel. Use "I feel..." statements as you engage in conflict with another person.

8) Learn how to stay separate energetically and in your own self-identity instead of feeling the other person's emotions in your body. This will assist you in being more clear and energized during and after your interaction.

9) Use positive affirmations when trying to change old ways of thinking or old beliefs. Louise Hay's book *You Can Heal Your Life* is all about this.

10) Remember GRATITUDE. Changing anything in your life will be easier if you practice this every day, and especially when working with your emotions. We all have many blessings in our lives and being grateful for these helps shift our attitudes as a whole. Some people think of what they're grateful for every night before going to sleep or every morning upon wakening. It doesn't matter how you do it, but gratitude will ease your soul and help you appreciate all that is.

"It is not the strongest of the species that survives, nor the most intelligent, but the one most responsive to change."
— *Charles Darwin*

Chapter 8

Solutions for a Healthier Lifestyle:
The Mind/Body Connection

My deep interest and belief is in the theory that each of us can greatly influence how and why we heal. This idea is what gives me hope and serves as the driver for the hard work and commitment it can take to heal. My job as a healer is to assist and empower my clients to heal themselves with all the tools that are available to them. The most powerful starting point is to involve our mind's abilities in the process of healing our bodies. I see myself as a co-creator with my client as we work together on whatever they bring to the table. It is not me who heals them, it is their own body, mind, and spirit being active or open enough to receive a healing signal when something is off balance, and their willingness to process whatever may have led them into this imbalance. It has been my experience that those who use their mind (thoughts and emotions), along with healing energy and sometimes other modalities, are able to heal on a level that sustains whatever has shifted in them. The many healing miracles that I have witnessed in my life have strengthened this deep belief in co-creation.

That said, there are many factors at play in healing. Sometimes people will not heal despite their dedicated efforts – and mine. I have seen the deep mystery of healing at work, and we cannot always control an outcome. Sometimes when a person is working with a difficult disease or with terminal illness they are able to heal deeply on many other levels before their passing, thus giving them a needed sense of clarity, acceptance and peace. This is no small thing, and is one of the many gifts that energy healing can bring. I have heard beautiful stories of gifted healers in hospice care who help bring their patients to this place of peace before their passing.

Early cultures such as ancient Egypt and Greece and many Eastern cultures had beliefs and practices that are based on a strong connection between mind, body and spirit. These beliefs resulted in the healing practices of yoga, meditation, tai chi, chi gung and more. We now have a growing field of research that supports the ancient understanding of this connection. The field of psychoneuroimmunology, which emerged about 40 years ago, studies the link between psychological factors and the activity of the immune system. It includes three main dimensions in its approach: psychology, neurology and immunology.

What follows is a brief history of the developments in the field of psychoneuroimmunology that support the connection between mind and body on which so many healing traditions are based. Later in this section I will give you practical applications for use on your personal journey of healing.

Using Your Mind to Heal Your Body

Psychoneuroimmunolgy, or PNI, is the study of the interaction between psychological processes and the nervous and immune systems of the body. The field also explores the benefit of many non-traditional, alternative or holistic approaches to medicine. The field of psychoneuroimmunology was named in 1975 by Dr. Robert Ader, who was the Director of Behavioral and Psychosocial Medicine at New York's University of Rochester. The basic premise of PNI is that there is a link between our thoughts and emotions and our ability to heal, and specifically, to affect our immune system functions.

One of the leaders in the development of the field of psychoneuroimmunology has been Joan Borysenko, Ph.D. She is the author of *The New York Times* best seller, *Minding the Body, Mending the Mind,* and also *The Power of the Mind to Heal.* She is the president and co-founder of Mind/Body Health Sciences, Inc., was an Instructor in Medicine at Harvard Medical School, and a former cancer cell biologist. Another leader, Dr. Esther Sternberg, is currently the Chief of the Section on Neuroendocrine Immunology and Behavior at the National Institute of Mental Health (NIMH). She is also the Director of the Integrative Neural Immune Program at the National Institute of Health. Dr. Sternberg is internationally recognized for her research on immune interactions and the brain's response to diseases including arthritis. Her book, *The Balance Within: The Science Connecting Health and Emotions*, and Joan Borysenko's books are the primary sources for the following summary description.

According to Borysenko, in the 1920s Dr. Walter Cannon, who was a professor of physiology at Harvard University, looked at the need for mental and physical balance throughout the human organism and coined the term "homeostasis," which means "similar position" in Greek. (similar in mind, similar in body) Cannon studied how emotions and perceptions register on the autonomic nervous system. Specifically, "negative" emotions affect the body's sympathetic and parasympathetic nervous systems by initiating the "fight or flight" response. You may have heard this term used in reference to people having a fear response. Dr. Cannon eventually found that emotions and diseases of emotions, or mental illness, could be seen as disturbances of the neurotransmitters and hormones.

At the same time in Canada, (according to Dr. Sternberg), the endocrinologist and physiologist Dr. Hans Selye, contributed significant research to the development of the field of PNI. While at

McGill University in the 1920s, Dr. Selye made an observation that led him to synthesize his theories of the generalized stress response. He researched animals that were put under adverse physical and mental conditions consistently and found that they adapted so they could heal and recover. He referred to this as "general adaption syndrome" and first wrote about it in 1936. He also found that during this adaption, the thymus, adrenals and other major organs of the immune system shrank if the stress in the environment was ongoing, and that eventually the animal would die.

What this means biologically is that when an animal is stressed, it releases a hormone called corticosterone. In humans this hormone is called cortisol, and when we have chronic stress, the pituitary gland in our brain secretes a hormone called adrenocorticotropin, or ACTH for short. This hormone binds to cells in the outer cortex of the adrenal glands, which causes them to manufacture and secrete cortisol. Under continual stress these glands will keep increasing in size as they are asked to make more and more cortisol. The hormone cortisol is a repair hormone when needed in the short term. But when continually produced, it becomes an immunosuppressant. In this case cortisol prevents the body from making new immune cells, and it inhibits the activities of the immune cells we already have in our body.

In 1945 Dr. Selye became the director of the Institute of Experimental Medicine at the Université de Montreal. Dr. Selye was responsible for introducing the word "stress" into the vocabularies of many different languages, as no word prior to that described it properly. He continued to do research around his theories on stress and its effects on health and created quite an uproar in the scientific community in the 1940s and 1950s. It took decades for the scientific community to give him credit for his theories on stress. As Esther Sternberg writes "It also took decades for the science of the immune and nervous systems to mature to the point where it could identify all the molecules and hormones that come into play when the two systems communicate. It wasn't until this communication was well understood that the phenomena that Selye so precisely and correctly observed in his rats in 1936 (and, as a medical student, in his patients in 1925) could be explained. It took another 40 years for immunologists to begin to believe that stress might make you sick in day-to-day circumstances through such hormonal mechanisms."

Dr. Selye along with Dr. Ader were two of the pioneers who researched how stress, hormones, emotions and the immune system were related. Over time and through the invention of new technologies, the inter-relatedness of these body systems became clearer.

According to Dr. Borysenko in her book, *The Power of the Mind to Heal*, Dr. Ader found in a study with mice that it is possible to "classically condition" the immune system. In the same way Pavlov taught dogs to salivate at the sound of a bell by associating two signals until the salivating behavior became automatic, "Dr. Ader and his colleague, immunologist Nicholas Cohen, showed that if rats were given an immunosuppressive drug accompanied by apple juice, later on the rats would immunosuppress just by tasting the juice. Rats could also be exposed to drugs that enhanced different aspects of the immune system, and the immunoenhancement could be similarly trained."

This demonstrates that any association that is "conditioned" can trigger both positive and negative effects on the immune system. This means that whether you are looking at a positive or negative trigger, you have a choice to be pro-active in conditioning yourself to achieve the outcome you are looking for.

In summary, the science of PNI says that:

1) Hormones released by our emotions and moods can cause an illness in the body.

2) Illness in the body can stimulate hormones that change our emotions and moods.

3) Though Western medicine once believed that pathogens are the cause of all disease, a great deal of

recent research suggests a more complicated situation. Much of the research is based on the neuroscience of the central nervous system and the neuroendocrine system and focuses on how the immune system communicates or interrelates with these systems.

In 1950 Dr. Sternberg's father was a professor of medicine at Université de Montreal along with Dr. Selye. All of this scientific study around young Esther Sternberg sparked her own curiosity about psychoneuroimmunology and related areas. She trained in rheumatology and practiced medicine in Montreal before returning to a research career and teaching at Washington University in St. Louis. Her research was in part an extension of Dr. Selye's work and other pioneers in the mind/body connection.

Dr. Sternberg writes about the body's automatic responses to emotions through our autonomic nervous system. When we are feeling an emotion, there is both a sensory end, which triggers an emotional response, and a motor end, the physical or physiological responses that we feel in our body. These happen when we feel fearful, anxious or angry or even when we're falling in love. Our bodies will respond in visceral ways to these emotions.

When we notice that we're sweating, or our gut is aching, or our heart is beating faster, we are not consciously making those things happen. They are automatically expressed through our autonomic nervous system. These reactions can happen whether the stressor is in front of us, or whether we are visualizing or thinking about the stressful event. In either case, the same hormonal and chemical responses will happen in the body. These hormonal responses that affect our immune responses are the connecting point between our health and our thought and emotions.

Dr. Sternberg also learned that memory influences our physical responses and the feelings that we are sensing. When our mood suddenly changes, it may be because a specific memory is triggered along with the emotions that were first connected to that memory. When we hear a song that reminds us of our first boyfriend/girlfriend it might bring us a happy, warm feeling or it could be a negative memory with feelings of anger, sadness or regret. Whether the stressors are large or small, our body/mind will respond by sending hormones throughout our system.

However, not everyone responds in the same way to stress. It appears that we all have a different "set point" for registering stress. Sternberg chronicles the findings of George Solomon, a psychiatrist at UCLA and one of the pioneers of psychoneuroimmunolgy, who showed that a situation does not need to be one that is a risk to life to be a real and potent stressor. Conversely, not all people who are involved in a situation where there is a risk to life perceive it to be a major stress. He and others measured immune and hormone responses in people who had been in the epicenter of the 1994 Northridge earthquake near Los Angeles within hours of the quake. Some people responded with high stress hormones and low immune responses, but others did not. The degree to which these people perceived themselves to be in a real danger could have been one of the factors that had something to do with these differences.

Another possibility for the differences is that some of the people in the study had many different stressors at the same time. People who care for children and simultaneously work full time, or those who've recently changed jobs or experienced a move or are in caregiver situations or similarly demanding activities, can develop "burnout" or what is literally extreme exhaustion. Some studies show that in addition to psychological burnout, these people may experience a physiological burnout. Their bodies have become unable to respond to any stress with even a slight burst of cortisol. Chronic stress can also change other hormone systems in the body, for example the reproductive hormones in both women and men can shut down. Dr. Sternberg suggests that we can recover from burnout with sufficient rest and reestablish our normal hormone levels and cycles. In some cases though, irreversible physical changes occur as a result of chronic stress.

Dr. Sternberg recounts recent research showing other factors involved in people's varied responses to stress. A psychologist at Mount Sinai School of Medicine named Rachel Yehuda found from caring for Holocaust survivors that their adult children had abnormal responses to stress, even though they had not experienced the Holocaust or war themselves. She tested the hormonal responses to stress of the survivors, their siblings, and children and found that they all had higher than expected cortisol rises in response to stress and lower resting levels of stress hormone rhythms throughout the day. She concluded that this response could either be something that was subconsciously learned by the children or that there is an inherited stress response. Whether passed through the genes or learned or both, these people responded more profoundly to a threat, and this was evidenced in their physiology.

An even earlier pioneer in this area, Candace Pert, PhD., was one of the first neuroscientists to recognize that the brain and the immune system might communicate at a molecular level. She is an internationally recognized neuroscientist and pharmacologist who has published over 300 scientific articles on peptides and their receptors and the role of these neuropeptides in the immune system. (Neuropeptides are the chemicals that allow the transmission of signals from one nerve to the next, sending messages back and forth.) She was Chief of Section on Brain Biochemistry of the Clinical Neuro-Science branch of the National Institute of Mental Health. She is also the author of the books, *Molecules of Emotion: the Scientific Basis Behind Mind-Body Medicine*, and *Everything You Need to Know to Feel Go(o)d*.

Through her research in the 1980s, Candace Pert discovered that neurotransmitters and neuropeptides are not only found in the brain, but they are also found on the cell walls of the immune system, all major organs, our muscles, glands, skin and tissue. There is a neurochemical response from our central nervous system with every thought, emotion, idea or belief. When strong emotions such as fear, anger, helplessness or hopelessness are not expressed outwardly, the body's natural response is to go into the "fight or flight" mode. When we feel one of these strong emotions but don't express it, we are not in "homeostasis," in which the body and the mind are "lined up." And when we don't express our negative emotions, the body produces an excess of epinephrine, which in turn causes a chemical breakdown, and results in internal weakening of the immune system, increasing the potential for disease. In contrast, positive emotions produce different chemicals like dopamine and serotonin.

Different parts of our brain control different emotions. Our amygdala controls fear and trauma, while the nucleus accumbens controls the positive emotions such as happiness, pleasure, comfort and the sexual responses that are associated with romantic love. The hypothalamus controls our physiological responses to the emotions controlled by either the amygdala or nucleus accumbens and does so automatically and with immediacy.

Dr. Pert believes that emotion is not fully expressed until it reaches a conscious place in our being, which she says includes the entire body. "I believe that unexpressed emotion is in the process of traveling up the neural access. By traveling, I mean coming from the periphery, up the spinal cord, up into the brain. When emotion moves up, it can be expressed. It takes a certain amount of energy from our bodies to keep emotion unexpressed. There are inhibitory chemicals and impulses that function to keep the emotion and information down. I think unexpressed emotions are literally lodged lower in the body."

Dr. Pert thinks there are levels of integration. We are integrating lower brain areas when we move the emotion up and get it into consciousness, which is where we begin to comprehend it. These unexpressed emotions are buried deep down in the circuitry of the organs or in a loop in the ganglium. Dr. Pert goes on to say that we even know what the memory storage of these emotions looks like. It involves protein molecules coupled up to receptors, and they can be seen in both the brain and body. So it is possible to see "stored memory" as protein molecules in a person's pancreas or kidney for instance.

The research at the core of PNI makes it ever more clear that our state of mind affects our ability to fight off infection and ill-health. For one doctor and surgeon this has become his life's work as he helps his patients heal themselves of cancer. Bernie Siegel MD writes in *Love, Medicine and Miracles* about his work with cancer patients:

The "surveillance" theory is one of the most widely accepted explanations of cancer. It states that cancer cells are always developing in our body but are normally destroyed by white blood cells before they can develop into dangerous tumors. Cancer will appear when the immune system becomes suppressed and can no longer deal with this routine threat. Because of the stress and tension that our present lifestyle seems to bring, we have a greater tendency to keep our stress response "on" for long periods of time or continually, and then the stress hormones lower our resistance to disease. It now appears through experimental evidence that "passive emotions" such as grief, feelings of failure and suppression of anger, produce oversecretion of these same hormones which suppress the immune system.

Thanks to the passage of time and the creation of new technology we can begin to understand the mysteries that occur in our brain and immune system that Hans Selye proposed 76 years ago. Now we can actually see on an MRI where the different parts of the brain light up when activated in particular sequences. In *The Balance Within*, Dr. Sternberg states that "Stress *can* make you sick because the hormones and nerve pathways activated by stress change the way the immune system responds, making it less able to fight invaders."

Mind – Body Healing

After learning about psychoneuroimmunology you may be thinking that you are a sitting duck for some sort of disease because of your stress level and the way you respond to it. And it could be something you need to look at. But if you are seeing it that way, see how that in itself is a thought form based in fear instead of opportunity. Instead, you could look at it through a more positive lens, which says that by learning this new information you have gained power. If you had not become aware of this connection, your body would still have responded accordingly. Now you can use this awareness for your benefit.

We have learned that the neuropeptides that are produced by our brain will vary depending on our emotions, which means that our immune system is listening to our mental talk (as well as what we actually say out loud) and is responding accordingly. Our thinking completely affects how we feel, so having a positive attitude is much more important than we may have thought. It is also true that our attitudes and beliefs can help us heal. Just the act of smiling produces hormones that are a positive boost to our immune system.

Even though we already have learned to associate certain behaviors around our health with certain outcomes, these too can shift through conscious awareness and experimentation. We are all able to learn new behaviors and make new and different connections between our feelings, actions and these outcomes. It is important to remember that WHENEVER you decide to change something in yourself, early or late in life, you will receive the benefit. Using the "I'm too old to do something different" rationalization is really just a cop out that means "I don't want to," which can be said at any age. We all have the choice to learn and grow and change, no matter where we are on our path. Change is not necessarily any easier to do when you're younger. It has more to do with the state of mind with which you take on the challenge.

Often change happens when we realize that letting our pain stay the same is harder than the effort it would take to change it. Sometimes finding that inner spark that gets us motivated comes by imagining how our life could be different if.... and then having the realization that change really is possible. The effort of change requires a strong desire, discipline, love of self, courage, and commitment to realizing the end goal. As with anything difficult in life, using humor is useful and recommended.

Let me summarize: Your body responds to the emotional heaviness or levity that you carry with you on a daily basis. It also responds to your thoughts, which are different from your feelings. Earlier in this book I spoke about how I've come to experience the body as responding to words very much like a four-year-old responds, rather simply and innocently receiving messages without much resistance. Literally, I mean when I ask a client's feet to open to the "earth energy" it will often immediately pour in, when a moment before that the person's feet were blocked from receiving the energy. Another example is when I ask a client to say out loud "I am free to speak my truth," and after doing so his or her throat chakra opens. We need to choose our words from a conscious place as much as possible, which I acknowledge is not easy to do, and is not possible to do all of the time. But the more we can speak consciously, the better.

Realizing that our thoughts are affecting our health may help us to decide to be more conscious. Thoughts are coming and going even more quickly than emotions, and my experience has shown that we have the ability to train them in certain directions. For example, when you notice yourself going down a path of negative thinking or self-critical thinking, you can say "cancel" or "I'm not going there" or just plain "no" to yourself and have a positive line in your memory waiting to replace the negative one such as "I love myself exactly as I am," or

"I am lovable," or something else to redirect yourself. To stop yourself and then redirect is a way of becoming conscious and centered in that moment and then choosing a different path. Find a statement prior to needing it, and one that resonates with you so that you are prepared for those times when you start to go down a path of negative mind chatter. We all have occasion to use this exercise, so take a moment now and see if you can find a positive affirmation that will be useful to you in the future. Some other affirmations might be "I am safe now and always," "I trust the flow of life," "I am a strong, capable person," or "I release all negativity and choose love instead." There are endless options for affirmations and I recommend using Louise Hay's book *You Can Heal Your Life* to find which ones pertain to you if you are uneasy making up your own (though I believe you could get the hang of it quickly).

Being more conscious about our thoughts and emotions will require major change for most of us. What it really means is retraining your brain. Let me suggest pausing several times a day to check in with yourself to see if you are on automatic pilot, or if you are aware of your thoughts and emotions. You could set your watch or phone for particular times throughout the day to remind yourself until it becomes a habit to stop and check in. It is a little frightening to find out that much of what we do each day is habit. When we do these habitual activities, like driving our kids to sports practice, or cooking dinner, we are most likely thinking all sorts of thoughts that may or may not be the best for us. We could choose to bring in a positive tone, an attitude of acceptance or kindness toward ourselves or others. The idea is to retrain our brains and literally create new neural pathways for ourselves. This can go a long way in creating a more positive atmosphere in which to live. When we pause, we also get more centered and grounded in our own true essence, which is where we find more joy, and this typically leads us to focus more on the positive than the negative. I love the quote, "Life is Change. Change is Optional. Choose Wisely." What it means to me is that things around us are always changing and that we can either adapt to that change or resist it. Typically our ability to adapt by expanding or growing is going to create a healthier environment than being resistant to "what is," since that is unlikely to go away.

Another way to become more conscious or aware of our thoughts and to train them to be more positive is through meditation. When we slow down our minds and let the thoughts go by instead of giving them attention, the mind learns to stop wandering. It takes practice, but it is quite useful and can change your life. While you are in meditation, fully centered and conscious, is a powerful time to give yourself whatever positive messages that you want to work on. For example if you're trying to work with a specific illness like pneumonia, you would bring in the thoughts or say the words out loud that your lungs are now opening up and clearing any mucous or blockage. You could simultaneously do breathing exercises that expand your lungs much more than a typical breath, as you're imagining or saying the words. Or if you'd like to be more trusting in the world you may use the meditation time to tell yourself that you are safe and protected wherever you are, or some other similar words that you can use as a sort of mantra to move yourself into a healthier mindset around trust. Or a person who would like to become less anxious and calmer instead could use a mantra that would speak to that. Giving yourself these kinds of messages while you are fully conscious and aware will have a positive effect on the neurotransmitters that are communicating inside of you with every thought and emotion that is registered and recorded in your cells.

When you would like to change something in yourself physically, emotionally or spiritually, it helps to get yourself in a conscious place either through meditation or by grounding and centering. By this I mean coming to a place where you feel calm, quiet and strong within yourself. (I go more deeply into this idea in the meditation section later in this chapter.) Whether it is working on a weakness or an emotion or just strengthening an aspect of yourself, it is useful to become fully aware of what you would like to change and find the best words to speak to yourself to bring in a new message and make yourself stronger in that area. Repeat them for days or weeks to fully bring in a new pattern. It takes a while to change pathways, as strong habitual behaviors create a deep "rut" in your brain, so you need to literally create a new pathway.

Remember that doing these exercises will strengthen your immune system as your neuropeptides (brain hormones) send positive chemicals throughout your body. Since we give ourselves negative messages at other times, we need to really focus on these positive ones when we're conscious in order to change our body chemistry or bring it back into a healthier balance. Doing these exercises does just that, and reminds us to focus on what gives us more energy instead of what takes energy away from us. This is a choice we make every moment of every day.

Two Laws of Energy

Healing teachers I've worked with have referred to two laws of energy that seem relevant here. The first one is that **Energy Moves With Intention**. What this means is that when you consciously use your intention, you gain the power to choose what you want to create and the ability to carry it out (like in the above affirmation exercise). What you intend to do can be done because you have declared it and moved your energy in that direction. This may mean writing out a step-by-step process to achieve a particular goal, or it may mean attracting the perfect person to you to help accomplish such a plan. If you focus on a particular goal or intention and do some imagery with it, such as "seeing" it happen (like athletes do to win gold medals), you are more likely to attract or magnetize important connections that will help you fulfill your intentions. (I detail the practice of visualization more fully later in this chapter.) We often get stuck in thinking that there is a certain way that something has to be done, and that can keep us from being awake enough to notice the unexpected gifts that are there for us, the "chance encounters."

The second law of energy is that **Whatever You Focus On Gets Bigger.** This is very important here, as we are trying to discern what kind of messages we want to give to ourselves day in and day out. We also need to realize what NOT to give our energy to. When we focus on how hard things are or compare ourselves to someone else, we are depleting our own energy. As I stated earlier, REFOCUSING our thoughts in a positive direction is what we need to do until we have lost the habit of putting ourselves down or other useless and destructive ideas. Instead we can take note of what we are grateful for, how well we managed a difficult situation, or how we responded in a new way that was rewarding. I'm sure you've heard this statement before: *It is not our circumstances that determine who we are, but how we see and respond to them that defines us.* Many people have lived through great difficulties and have found miraculous ways to thrive in the face of it. What do those people have that some of us do not? Well, at the very least they have courage and hope, and those two states of mind help them to see difficulty as a challenge or to look at it with a positive frame of reference instead of with despair. It is more likely that people with courage and hope will be successful at coping well. And now we know through research that when we learn to cope successfully we move toward better health because as we cope we are strengthening instead of weakening our immune systems.

Questions about your mind/body relationship

1) Have you ever thought that your emotions and attitudes may be linked to your health?

2) Are you aware of certain areas of your thinking that you would like to change?

3) What beliefs are keeping you from moving forward?

4) How would you gauge your stress level in the past day? week? month? year?

5) Do you think your stress level is contributing to lack of health?

6) Do you feel that you are good at coping with difficulties that come your way?

7) Do you cope by denying or ignoring emotions?

8) Are you more prone to positive or negative self-talk?

9) Would you like to be more conscious of your mind chatter?

10) What is a habit or pattern you would like to put LESS energy into?

11) Do you respond to circumstances with fear or anger very often?

12) How could you respond differently?

13) Do you think of problems as failures or do you prefer to see them as a challenge?

14) Do you respond to things with a positive attitude generally?

15) Do you trust and follow your intuition very often?

16) Can you accept yourself the way you are, even with your imperfections?

17) What would be some useful affirmations for you?

When you want to use your mind to help with the healing of a specific health issue, such as cancer, it is realistic to expect that you will need courage and a willingness to go out of your comfort zone to learn things that have always been a part of your unconscious nature. There are several tools in this toolbox to use, but your own perseverance and determination is what will really make the difference. A healer can help bring these unconscious patterns to the surface, but digging in will be yours to do. Bringing in a strong will, flexibility and positive attitude is what often brings people back into a balanced state of health. It is a process of learning, growing and healing on a deep level that can change or affect all aspects of your life. I've never known anyone who went through this process who wished they hadn't, regardless of their outcome.

Later in the book, I will illustrate this chapter's message through the story of a dear friend who was diagnosed with breast cancer in February of 2011. My friend Jane told me about her diagnosis immediately upon learning about it and asked me if I would help her through her healing of this cancer. Jane's story is a perfect example of mind and body healing.

"We are at peace with God and all mankind when we hear the silence and do not feel alone."
— *Unknown*

Meditation

Meditation is probably one of the single best things you can do for healing yourself because doing it affects all areas – mind, body and spirit. There are several purposes of meditation which we will discuss in this chapter, but one is to quiet and empty your mind. Think of all the stimulation you receive on a daily basis. There is a constant stream of information coming at each of us, and this is increasing with more technology and the quickened pace of our lives. Meditating can allow you a period of time to completely stop all of this input and just be present to yourself. Your mind gets overloaded and cluttered throughout the day, and like a computer, the disc can just become full. When I feel that I cannot receive any more input, I meditate "to clear the slate" and give myself a fresh start. Doing so really helps me go back into the world grounded and centered so I can function better.

There are many types of meditation or ways to meditate, including mindfulness meditation, grounding meditation, focusing completely on your breath, or chanting a mantra. There is no right or wrong way. No matter what type you practice, it is healing for your body as well as your mind and spirit to meditate regularly. One main objective is to slow down enough so that we are able to reconnect with the silence in ourselves. There is so much input around us that we can feel like we don't know who we are, or what is at our center. Facing ourselves in silence is what brings us back to that core, or what I like to call our "Divine Essence."

We used to believe that somewhere between 20 to 25 years of age, the brain was finished with growth and development. But recent meditation (and other neuroscience) research suggests that is not the case. Now that we have improved technology for seeing the brain and studying the effects of meditation, it has become clear how beneficial meditation can be. In an article in *Shambala Sun* (July 2011), Michael Baime discusses how modern neuroscience explains the way meditators experience life by changing the physiology of the brain. Dr. Baime is Clinical Associate Professor of Medicine at the University of Pennsylvania, at the Abramson Cancer Center in Philadelphia. He founded the Penn Program for Mindfulness in 1992 and is involved in projects exploring the effects of mindfulness and meditation. According to Baime, "the most recent research suggests that a regular (daily) meditation practice can cause beneficial structural changes in the brain in as little as eight weeks." In this same article, Baime summarizes research done by Sara Lazar, a Harvard neuroscientist, who looked at the outermost surface of the brain called the cortex. She found that some cortical areas in the brains of meditators, as opposed to a control group, were significantly thicker. The cortex atrophies with age, but in Lazar's meditating subjects these enlarged areas were the same thickness as that measured in nonpractitioners twenty years younger. In previous studies it was shown that the prefrontal cortex and the insula were more active during meditation practice. (See *Shambala Sun*, July 2011, to read more and to see photos of the brain scans taken before and after meditation.)

In addition to positive changes within our brains, research has shown that meditation can lower heart rate, help normalize blood pressure, lower the level of stress hormones in the blood, and deepen oxygen intake in the body. David Servan-Schreiber MD, PhD cites several studies on meditation in his book *Anti-Cancer: A New Way of Life.* One study conducted by Jon Kabat-Zinn found that even with beginners, those who meditated every day for eight weeks had significant changes in the electrical activity of their brains as measured by an electro-encephalogram (EEG). The regions of the brain that were associated with positive mood and optimism were distinctly more active compared to their earlier state or to that of the control group. In this study all of the participants were also given the flu vaccine, and the immune systems of those who meditated reacted more forcefully to the vaccine than those of the members of the control group.

Some people who meditate regularly like to use a mantra. The following research shows how the body can be affected positively by using a mantra. Dr. Servan-Schreiber cites another study done by

Luciano Bernardi, MD, PhD of the University of Pavia in Italy. Dr. Bernardi's interest is in the autonomous body rhythms that form the foundations of physiology: Variations in heart rate, blood pressure, respiration, etc. He knew that a sound balance between these various bio-rhythms is perhaps the most accurate indicator of good health. Dr. Bernardi had his subjects recite a stream of *Ave Marias* in Latin and found that his subjects' biological rhythms started to resonate. They all lined up, one after the other, mutually amplifying one another to create a smooth, harmonious pattern. Dr. Bernardi then had another set of subjects do a mantra from Buddhism: *Om Mani Padme Hum*, and he found that these subjects responded similarly. Their breathing automatically adopted a pace of six breaths a minute, a harmonization or coherence with the rhythms of the other autonomous physiological functions.

Dr. Esther Sternberg and Julian Thayer published an article in the *Annals of the New York Academy of Sciences* (2006) about their study of the amplitude or size of a wave motion (or in this case bio-rhythms) and variations of biological rhythms. (The amplitude of biological rhythms is the greatest at birth and the lowest at death, declining approximately 3 percent a year.) They concluded that everything that amplifies (or increases) variations - as happens in the states of resonance or "coherence" described by Bernardi - is associated with a number of health benefits. *In particular they found better functioning of the immune system, reduction of inflammation, and better regulation of blood sugar levels.* (These are three of the principal factors that act against the development of cancer.) This coherence or balance is also one of the biological functions that responds best to training your breathing and concentration, and is exactly what Dr. Bernardi discovered through his subjects who practiced the ancient Buddhist mantra and the rosary.

When we are in states of stress, anxiety, anger or depression the natural variation in cardiac rhythm becomes weak or irregular or "chaotic." Conversely when we are in states of well-being, compassion, or gratitude, or when we focus our attention on breathing, the variability of our cardiac rhythm is greater and becomes "coherent." Whether we are meditating, reciting a mantra or prayer, or just focusing on our breath, we are able to bring our biological rhythms into a harmonious or coherent state that will bring about the above-mentioned health benefits. The more often we are in this state, the better it is for our body/mind.

It appears to me that being in this coherent state allows certain areas of our body to take in energy where there is an imbalance, so that healing can take place. Most of us do the bulk of our healing work on our bodies as we sleep. But if we take time out of our day to sit down and meditate, and focus on bringing energy into our body, we are giving it a gift that our cells will respond to. As Deepak Chopra says, meditation is a time that we begin the process of creating new, healthy cells to take the place of the diseased ones. If we send positive messages to ourselves about our ability to heal, and even visualize the change, our body has the opportunity to respond.

Many people who meditate regularly have a certain space to do it in that they make sacred with an altar or special objects that are spiritual for them. This isn't necessary though, and I find that I can meditate in any number of places just fine, especially outside. We can do centering meditation, mindfulness meditation, walking or moving meditation (like Tai Chi), we can focus on bringing in earth energy, we can focus on a certain body part to heal, we can work on connecting to our hara (our center of spiritual power), or just notice what is there and let it be there. No matter what type of meditation we do, we want to bring attention to our self and our silence within, either with a specific intention, a certain prayer, or just by completely clearing the mind.

If you have never done meditation before, I recommend beginning the practice of it by taking a class. It may be that you'll want to try several types to find the one that is right for you. I wouldn't try to do it from a book, at least at the beginning, because you will get discouraged and probably give it up. Meditation requires discipline (something that may be getting lost in our current culture), courage, and perseverance.

One of the gifts of being in a class is that it allows you to realize how hard it is for *everyone*. A good teacher will tell you that meditation is about the practice of sitting there and not about the outcome. That is something in and of itself that is useful. When you get frustrated, you just move on, with compassion instead of judgement of yourself, and keep attempting to quiet the mind until the next thought comes in. With practice (and maybe a lot of it), you can get to a place of no thought. It is a beautiful place where your mind is truly quiet; meaning that once you are aware of your mind being quiet or not being quiet, the moment has passed. It feels like nothingness and perfect inclusion all at once. While you're in this state there is somehow an underlying awareness of how you "fit" into the grand scheme of the universe. One teacher I had said that you realize that what is inside of you and outside of you are the same. Once you return from your meditation, your thoughts will usually feel very calm and less reactive. Being in a group with the energy of others meditating around you will enhance your ability to reach the place you would like to be in with more ease.

I tried meditating on my own for ten years without any instruction, and it was never easy to get beyond the "monkey mind" (continual swirling thoughts). Once I took some classes, my meditation deepened, and soon I was able to be completely without thought and feel very deeply rested from my meditations. As a hint, it was connecting with the earth energy and feeling it come up into my feet and body that helped me stay out of my head. It became more of a body experience and that allowed the quiet to take place. Later I will instruct you in a grounding meditation, the type of meditation that I continue to practice and teach.

The feeling that I get in meditation when I reach the place I strive for is one of "connecting up." This means there is a line (my *hara* line) that runs through the center of my body and goes into the core of the earth below me, and up to the divine (or heaven) above me, linking me up with all that is. Imagine a thin tubular straw-like shape that extends from the core of the earth, through my body and continues out the top of my head, going up to create my connection with God or the Divine. When this happens, my mind goes blank, and I receive the energy from this place of connection. I feel as if I'm in an altered state, in another consciousness, as there is no conscious thought while I'm in this place. Time is lost, and I have no memory of what goes on there once I return to regular consciousness. When I return from it, I feel a deep sense of well-being, satisfied and relaxed, grounded and centered, and often energized.

Maybe the most important benefit from meditation is that it brings us back to our "Divine Essence," our spiritual nature, over and over again. This is our Godself or higher self, and I think it is when we get away from this place for too long that we run into problems. The imperfection of human nature comes in, and we act in ways that we are not proud of or happy about. I need to meditate regularly to be connected to my best qualities. It helps me remember my strengths, be aware of my weaknesses, and learn to accept or make a positive shift in my attitudes and choices. This awareness allows me to consciously choose how I will behave.

"We must truly know ourselves before we can begin to know the truth."

— *Unknown*

A General Meditation Exercise

To begin, find a comfortable, quiet place where you will be free from outer distractions.

- Turn off your phone and computer and anything else that may distract you so your focus can be clearly on connecting with yourself and quieting your mind.

- To be physically comfortable there are a couple positions I can suggest. The first is to sit in a chair that is conducive to keeping your back/spine straight, your neck slightly lifted, and your feet flat on the ground, with nothing crossed (arms or legs). This is an especially suitable position for connecting with the earth energy as it allows the flow of it to come up into your feet and then move up and through you.

- The second position would be to sit cross-legged on the floor, on a prayer pillow, or a meditation stool or with a pillow under you so that your back can still be straight and upright. Regardless of which position you choose, I do NOT recommend learning to meditate while lying down. Most of us are sleep deprived and we will just go to sleep. Even the most practiced meditators do not usually lay down unless they're ill and that's the only position they can meditate in.

- Once you have found a comfortable position, always begin by taking several deep breaths. It might take three and it might be better to do more, but this is a good way to start. Focus your attention on your breath and notice how your abdomen expands as you use diaphragmatic breathing. This means to fill your abdomen first, pushing it outward and then fill up your lungs by expanding them completely, then exhale backwards by releasing the upper lungs, lower lungs and your abdomen last as you pull it back in toward your back.

- Next you can feel how the air touches your nostrils on its way in and then on your exhale. This will help bring your focus to what is going on in the moment and keep you from getting distracted by your mind. You may also wish to focus on releasing anything you no longer need in that moment with every exhalation. For example, allow yourself to blow out any stress or tension that you may feel in your mind or body as you exhale. You may also choose to breathe something in, like peace or calm, with every inhalation. Another powerful way to bring yourself in contact with your deepest self is to say internally or out loud your **full** name to yourself three times. For example: "I am (*state your full name here*)."

- After you have settled into yourself you can let go of your consciousness around your breathing and just breathe in what is a natural flow for you. Undoubtedly you will find your mind having thoughts because that is what it does. You can either tell yourself that you will bring back that line of thinking when you are done with the meditation (if it's important), or you can just let the thoughts go, realizing that what you're thinking probably does not need to be revisited and it was just the normal mind play that happens to us. It is extremely useful to be a curious observer, just noticing but not attaching to what comes in as thought, nor judging it in any way as good or bad, valid or useless, just as a thought that is present. When we can really do this, we train ourselves to become more aware of what is going on inside and we become less reactive. This is one of the gifts that our meditation practice can bring to our normal, waking state. This is how we expand our consciousness to strengthen the shifts in ourselves as we move through our lives. We want to notice what is coming to our attention and say "this is what is happening now," accept it, and leave it at that as we meditate. We can then begin to use this practice as a way of changing those habits that cause us to be unhappy for whatever reason when we're in our usual awake state. Our habits can change because our brain is forming new neural pathways during meditation that will lead us to fewer disharmonies.

- When we can just notice, for example the emotion of fear, we can sit with it, not believing we shouldn't be having it, because it is what is present. Instead, we experience being with the feeling of fear, maybe exploring it in this state without commenting on its existence, but more in an open state of reflection and curiosity. To move through an emotion, all we need is to have compassion for ourselves for being human, for feeling fear or loneliness or grief. If we can give this to ourselves as we can for a loved one, we may watch the emotion shrink. If the pain stays as you watch it, then so it is. It is probably telling you something, and being in this quiet state is a good time to ask it what message it has for you. Whether this is a physical or emotional pain, you may receive an answer that may wisely address this pain to help move you in a direction that can heal it. So ask yourself the question and see what comes to you. This is another gift of meditation. We learn about ourselves while in this state. We learn about our tolerance or lack of it. We learn about how compassionate or loving we can be. We learn what is hardest for us to change about ourselves and what is easiest. We learn about our faith in ourselves and in the world.

- As you sit, you may completely lose your consciousness to your thoughts over time, but when necessary you may need to tell yourself to literally "cancel" that thought, using your will momentarily to push the thought out of your mind. You may also try focusing on one word, like joy or peace or calm, over and over, so your mind has something to do without attaching to anything else. Some people like to count until their mind is quiet.

- We all find our tricks for keeping our mind quiet for as many moments as possible. Even in the shortest time we can see glimpses of ourselves acting or feeling differently, like an "aha" moment, when we see a truth that we have not seen before. These will come more and more frequently as we continue to practice meditation. Not many people can sit down and meditate without distractions unless they have been practicing it for many, many years. Even then, to be human is to ebb and flow constantly and instead of focusing on your success or failure, it is best to accept your nature as it is in this moment, knowing that it will change the next time you sit down to meditate. Some meditations go easier than others, but all of them give us something.

- Another possibility I like to offer to people in meditation is to focus on a part of themselves that needs love and/or healing in that moment. It could be a physical pain in your body or even a disease, or it could be that you would like to focus on opening your heart or bringing in more patience. You can use your inhalation to bring in whatever your intention is and your exhalation to anchor it in the tissue, an organ, or your mind. This is a nice way to give yourself something specific before you end your practice. Keep in mind that any living being grows and learns best with gentleness, kindness and compassion. You deserve your love of self, your acceptance of self, and this is how you will best flourish.

Grounding Meditation

A Grounding Meditation helps you become more fully in your body. Before I give you an example of a Grounding Meditation, let's learn about the importance of earth energy so that you can understand the benefits that come from grounding your body. Grounding in these terms means connecting to and filling up with the earth's energy. This energy is like a battery that recharges your body. As you begin, this may feel like the lower part of your body is becoming heavy. You may also experience tingling or heat in your legs and feet, or even throughout your whole body. This is feedback telling you that you are actually receiving the earth energy. (You do not have to be outside or literally "on the ground" to do this meditation.)

Earth energy feeds all living things. All of life grows "up" from the earth. It needs to be grounded or rooted into the earth, whether it is a plant, a tree, an animal or a human being. This connection to the earth is the way we recharge our body's energy, and also the way we stay sane to some degree because it keeps us present in our body. You may have seen people who look like they are not in their body. It is as if they are not behind their eyes; they look lost. Those people are not grounded and they are most likely having difficulty in their lives. The deeper we go into the earth's energy (which has a lower vibrational frequency than we do) with our energy body, the stronger base we have. The earth's energy acts as an anchor and this allows us to hold more of the higher frequency energy that comes from above, or from the Divine (spirit energy). Those of us who work with energy realize that if we connect with earth energy to do healing work, it will be unlimited, whereas if we use energy from the heavens only, or what some might call "spiritual" energy, there is the possibility of burning out and even damaging our energy system because of the higher frequency of energy coming into us. (We would need to systematically build up to higher amounts of this high-frequency energy to use it exclusively, meaning not along with the earth energy.)

A Grounding Meditation Exercise

- To begin the meditation sit in a chair that allows you to keep your spine straight. Sometimes it is helpful to sit at the front edge of a straight back chair, but whether using pillows or your back muscles, sit up as straight as you can. You can imagine a string that is attached to the top and middle of your head that is pulling your head up gently so that your chin is parallel to the floor.

- Keep your feet flat on the floor or ground with no crossing of arms or legs as that blocks the flow of energy that comes up from the earth and into your feet and then goes throughout your body. Even if you are inside of a building, or even on the fiftieth floor of a building, you can still receive earth energy through your feet.

- Always begin by taking some deep cleansing breaths, meaning deeper than your usual day-to-day breathing. (Humans usually take in only half of their full lung capacity when they breathe!) Ask yourself to breathe out any stress or tension that you are holding inside of you. It is time to let it all go and focus on being present with your body, mind and spirit. So bring yourself fully into the space you are in, leaving behind all the details of your day. Let go of your work day, your drive home, your hectic moments, let them all be released through your breath as you become fully present in your body.

- Feel your feet on the ground and your bottom touching the chair, and all the boundaries of your body which are you. Just FEEL yourself. Notice what is present within you. Maybe you feel some pain, or you remember that you're angry with someone, or that you have a huge project that must be done. Acknowledge all of these things and then ask them to be set aside momentarily. You can come back to them when you're done with the meditation.

- Then again, take a deep breath and feel your feet. Rub your feet back and forth on the ground in front of you to stimulate the bottoms of them. There is a place on the ball of your foot that is about a third of the way down from the top of the toes. There is actually a small indentation here that you can feel with your fingers. This place is called "bubbling spring" in Chinese Medicine and it is also a kidney point. This is the place where our body opens up to take in earth energy; literally our own bubbling spring opens to restore our energy. When we consciously ask our body to take energy in through our feet, it becomes easier as we create a stronger, habitual pathway. All energy moves with our intention, so directing energy up through our feet intentionally on a regular basis will help create a stronger energy body and physical body.

- So you are now focusing on that spot on your feet and asking your feet to open and be receptive to receiving the earth's energy. Then imagine sending down from that place on your feet some roots that will go through all the layers of the earth; through the dirt, the rocks, the water and the fire, all the way down until those roots get to the core of the earth where the molten lava is. Then ask yourself to bring that earth energy up through all of those layers with your roots as a messenger that then delivers the earth energy into your feet. Bring that energy into your feet and then begin to pull it up into your ankles. If you are a visual learner, you may choose to bring in a color with the energy. Use the color red as that is the color of the first chakra and the vibration of life force energy.

- After you feel the sensation in your ankles, continue to

move the energy up through your calves until you feel a sensation there. Then bring the energy up your thighs, and then into your hips where you will anchor that energy into what we call the first chakra or energy center, which is from front to back between your pubic bone and your sacrum and from side to side between your hip bones. (The section on chakras gives you the colors for all the chakras if you want to visualize bringing each color to each chakra while focusing on it to strengthen it.) At this point you may be feeling heat or warmth, tingling or heaviness especially in your lower body, or super-relaxed in parts of your body that were tense before. These are just some of the sensations you may notice as energy moves into areas of your body.

- As you practice you may wish to continue bringing this energy up into your torso until you feel it reach your heart. At this point, I like to bring down the energy of the Divine or "God" energy from above your head and bring it in through the top of your head. From here you will use your intention to move it through your head and throat, and then meet up with the Earth energy in the heart. These two energies will intermingle, and by this time you may feel fairly deep in meditation and even be in an altered state where your mind can become quiet.

- Let go of all conscious thoughts now and just allow yourself to be in this place where your personal divinity is meeting with the energy from the earth and dancing with it. You may choose to direct yourself to do one more thing. Allow your eyes to softly focus (though staying shut) on the space between your eyebrows, which is also called your third eye. Focusing on this area can sometimes help your mind turn off, so you feel completely at peace, with no thoughts. Of course you don't know you have been in this place until you shift back and notice that peaceful and completely empty space is gone. But it can be exciting to reach this place of no thought, just true connection and oneness with all that there is. This is the place we all are hoping to get to; some will and some won't, but with practice it is available to all of us.

- If you have reached this empty and blissful state, then you need do no more. Again, if not, you may choose to calm your mind of thoughts by focusing on a word or mantra that you can say over and over again, or you may say to yourself "cancel", meaning to let go of any thoughts that are going around and around in your mind. Sometimes giving your mind something simple and repetitive to do will keep you from thinking about what you need to do at the meeting you are attending in the near future, or your child's cold. Another thing would be to breathe in while saying one word like *love*, and out while saying something else that you wish to release like *impatience.* All of these "games" are to help us become freed in allowing our mind to move as it will, but not letting it get stuck on any one thought. Even more importantly, our purpose here is just to let everything be as it is without attempting to judge it or change it. We are just learning about compassion and gentleness for ourselves and others and learning to not attach to what goes through our mind.

When you are finished with your meditation, notice the difference in yourself from before and after the meditation. You will likely feel calm, quiet, content and physically relaxed. It is usually a feeling that is pleasurable and will hopefully entice you to come back soon to yourself in another meditation.

Visualization

There are some tools we can use to focus the mind and use it for our benefit to create a healthier way of thinking and emoting. They can be used for a variety of purposes: Becoming more calm and centered, relaxing and getting more clear with our emotional life, assisting our body to function at its optimum capacity or to work directly with physical challenges or disease. Meditation, relaxation, visualization (sometimes called imagery) and hypnosis are ways to bring about change in these areas.

Relaxation can be formal or informal, meaning on your own or guided. There are a plethora of relaxation tapes/CDs out there, each with its own means of getting you to relax. One common practice is to tighten and then relax each part of your body, starting at the feet and going all the way up to the neck/head area. With each area you flex or tighten and then take a deep breath in, exhaling as you relax and settle into that body part. It may take a while to complete the whole body if you really are intent on relaxing everything. Often this is used for helping someone get to sleep if they are having a hard time. Or it can be used at the beginning of a meditation to get you into your body, relaxed and less aware of your mind.

It turns out that visualization, imagery and hypnosis are for all intents and purposes one and the same, but involve slightly different methods. They basically provide a way to use a positive image to change the way something currently is, or more specifically to heal an issue of mind, body or spirit. The image(s) may be used over and over again to assist in working toward something in particular or a vision of an end result. Sometimes a visualization only needs to be used once in the context of a prayer or meditation, and that may be all it takes to move you in a new direction. Hypnosis is usually done with a trained therapist who guides you through the process or you can learn self-hypnosis from a professional. Visualization, imagery and relaxation can be done alone or with assistance.

A Visualization Exercise

- To begin the process of visualizing (images), start by relaxing and going into meditation so your mind becomes emptied and receptive. This helps your mind become open to the power of suggestion and the full use of your imagination. For better or for worse, our minds cannot tell the difference between an actual physical experience and a vivid mental experience. (Think of how real a dream can seem to be.) This is the advantage we are using in invoking powerful images to help create a shift in us.

- Once you have become fully relaxed through meditation, find an image that you can see very clearly and one you are very comfortable using to create the change that you are looking for. Then focus on it.

- To strengthen the process, add positive words to go along with the actual visualization.

Let me illustrate with an example. My niece had a surgery that left her with unexplained problems in a major nerve in her leg. After increasingly excruciating pain, it was determined that she should receive intravenous steroids for twelve weeks, starting with three treatments the first week. When she came back from the hospital after her first treatment, she told me how she felt like poison was going into her and that it made her feel very anxious and afraid. I suggested that before she returned in two days for the next treatment, she could practice using visualization so that the next time her focus would be on how the treatment could benefit her fully. She came up with an image of a beautiful blue color calming the nerve and cooling down the inflammation. I also told her that it was important that she see this chemical as positive and one that would take away her pain and help her leg heal more quickly. She needed to somehow befriend these steroids so they could work for her and not against her.

Rev. Rosalyn Bruyere told me a story about research on people using chemotherapy and how the effects of a drug can change dramatically depending on one's feelings about the use of the drug. It was very similar to my niece's story because many people view chemotherapy as poison (which it is in one sense, but it can also save your life) and in this study they were practicing visualization techniques to tell their bodies it would be good for them. Those who did the visualization practice had more positive outcomes by having less side effects, more destruction of the cancer cells, and in some cases needing fewer chemo treatments than those who did not do the visualization. It is a way we can assist the body by participating in a positive manner toward something that may be "the least of the evils" or a necessary step in limited options for healing something.

My niece practiced her imagery and worked with her feelings about the steroids before she went to her next treatment. When she returned after her second intravenous treatment, she said it went much better and that she felt relaxed. She had used the imagery which helped her overcome her anxiety and discomfort about the whole process. She even went a step further by regularly visualizing and focusing on her injured nerve healing more quickly than the usual one inch per month.

Using visualization and imagery is basically directing your intention to change something in your life. To be successful, become conscious of what is happening whether you are working on an emotional, spiritual or physical aspect of your being, and create the desire to change. The focus is on what you want to happen or what you want to become. This exercise of mind, body and spirit healing is easier to carry out when one has a loving connection to self. Conversely, using these practices of meditation, visualization/imagery and hypnosis are ways to increase that loving connection to self.

Chapter 9

Solutions for a Healthier Lifestyle:
Addressing Your Psyche

Loving Yourself

When is the last time that you said to yourself that you are a good person and that you love who you are? Just reading this will probably make some of you feel nervous. So just stop and take a few deep breaths and feel your body. Feel your feet on the floor and listen to your breath until you feel calm and fully present.

Now ask yourself again, "Do I love myself?" and see what comes up for you. Do you think "Yes, I love myself," or "I don't know if I love myself," or "No, I don't love myself." Or maybe you just feel resistance to the whole thing. With compassion, be a curious observer, like a scientist collecting data, and just notice how you respond. Do you feel discomfort? Do you feel angry or nervous? Do you feel a happy glow inside? As you check this out, what words are coming into your mind? Become conscious of what your responses might mean and see if you can glean any wisdom from them. There could be an important message here for you, one that shows you a path that until now has been unknown to you.

From all my experience in working with people during classes or client sessions, the one thing I see over and over again, and that kind of surprises me, is how few people actually feel they love themselves. So if you are in this category, you are NOT alone. You are in good company.

The question is WHY? Why is it that so many of us do not feel that we love ourselves? This is really an important question to solve because there are many who believe that the ability to love ones self is at the core of health and healing, or the lack of healing. It is also very often an unconscious thought form. So let's bring it into the conscious arena so that you can determine what the messages are that keep you from feeling love for yourself, if that is the case.

Questions around self-love

1) Do you think that self-love means being narcissistic or vain? Why?
2) Do you think you have to be perfect to love yourself?
3) Do you think that all people have to be perfect to deserve love?
4) Do you think that anyone is really perfect?
5) Did someone tell you that you were unlovable? If so, who and why?
6) Why do you still believe that person (if that is the case for you)?
7) Have you done something that you cannot forgive yourself for, or have not yet forgiven yourself for doing?
8) Are you afraid of your power (and abilities) or of what you might actually accomplish if you loved yourself?
9) Do you feel it is unsafe to love anyone, including yourself?
10) Can you stop judging yourself and give yourself positive messages instead?

I realize these are intense questions. They get at the core of who we are, or the core of our personalities, and that is not always easy to look at. If you are having a hard time with this exercise, please bring in compassion for yourself. Treat yourself like a good friend by being very loving, accepting and kind. You are a gift from God or the Universe (whatever term makes you more comfortable), and you have a right to be here and a purpose for being here. Even if you don't know what that purpose is at this moment, it is true. We all get lost sometimes and need to regroup and find our way back to our own divine essence. There is no shame in losing our way; it is called being human. Being human is a messy business, not always good looking, fun or easy. Some would say it isn't for the faint of heart, and I would agree.

But here we are on this earth together, and if we are able to give and receive love more easily, I believe our journeys will lighten up for us all. Hopefully we can become less serious and use humor a lot more often. What if we could play more and work less and really enjoy the things we do each day? How would that change our lives? I believe that loving ourselves could be the basis for some of these things to happen. We spend too much time pushing other people away because we are afraid of getting too close. I think it is so they won't see that we are imperfect, but actually, so are they. If we could open our hearts and accept people as they are, and ourselves as we are, we would all end up loving more and being less fearful, and I believe this would make us much healthier people.

When we consciously choose self-love we inevitably give ourselves the things we need to be vibrant, happy, healthy people. This would include giving ourselves good food, exercise we like, positive messages, loving people in our lives, having satisfying spiritual practices and whatever else we feel we need to bring out the best in us. This sounds like common sense and yet, it is not a concept that is typically at the forefront of our conscious mind. Maybe that is because it requires work to think through and act on one's own behalf, and many of us don't think we should have to work that hard on our health and well-being.

To that I would suggest that anything worth having is worth working for, especially a healthy mind/body/spirit.

When we know that we feel self-love, we are generally happier, more powerful and therefore more productive people, and usually more flexible, loving and kind. It isn't, "I love me, I'm so great!"; it's more like, "I love and accept myself with all of my imperfections, my humanity." Loving yourself involves having compassion and humility and realizing that faith and forgiveness will pull you through the times when you didn't act as you wish you would have.

It also means that you care enough about yourself and others to regularly take a self-inventory for the purpose of noticing, and then confronting, those attitudes and behaviors that are not helpful in relationships and in your life in general. To be able to say "I'm sorry" or "I need help with this" is an important part of being human. Many of us find it very hard to acknowledge when we have failed at something or to make restitution in one way or another. We are ultimately responsible for our behavior and for changing our behavior if it is destructive or hurtful to ourselves or others. Our self-deception will not bring us joy or help our relationships. I would say everyone has plenty of "character flaws" they could become aware of in themselves that would be useful to change. Doing so requires courage and determination and usually perseverance. Our habits are imbedded in the fabric of our being, and it will most likely be difficult to make these shifts, but it is not impossible, and your life could have more meaning and pleasure from some serious self work. If you tend to go into guilt or shame when faced with these imperfections, it will likely freeze you up. In those moments you will probably not be able to make the kind of changes that are necessary. Feeling victimized, helpless or blaming others will also keep you from the real work of changing. Once you can hold both the negative behavior and the new, more positive behavior in your mind it will become more possible to choose which one you would like to inhabit. It is more likely that you will work on changing yourself if you feel a basic love of self than if you do not, because it feels like an investment in making your future better instead of just a hard thing to do.

Having the belief that it is possible for you to change yourself internally may be a necessary first step in consciously shifting to a healthier lifestyle, which is an act of self-love. I know of many who think people cannot change, and my first thought about that is that they don't think *they* can change. Because if they had experienced change in themselves then they would know that it can happen. Over the years I have seen others change in many ways, and I myself have changed over the years as well, so I believe that it is possible for people to change.

I don't think I could have the career I have without believing that people can change. That is the basis for the work I do, and not only have I witnessed bodies changing, but also people's emotional, mental and spiritual lives as well. Having this belief also gives me courage, strength and the will to keep working on myself. It allows me to wonder about the hard things in life and in myself and work on how I can make them better for my family, my community and myself. Most importantly it reveals my faith in people and the universe, and my belief that there is some order and meaning to our struggles and suffering. I believe that there is a loving force that governs the Universe (some may call this God) and that people are generally good.

I also believe that we all have a dark side that can be kept in check by our awareness and consciousness. It can and does become dangerous when it stays in the unconscious part of us and is not dealt with openly, or when we hate ourselves. Our pain may be so great that we are afraid someone might see our weaknesses or perceive our unbecoming thoughts, and so we hide them from others, not expressing or questioning them or processing them with someone we love. Maybe we feel horrible about certain behaviors we have engaged in but don't feel we have the power to change them. This brings us back to a lack of self-love and self-acceptance, and the inability to be compassionate and forgiving of our own imperfections or undesirable behaviors, which can keep us living with habitually poor self-care.

Just for a moment, even if you still feel resistance, let us agree that it is very important to learn to love yourself. And realize that if you can become friends with this idea, all of the information in this book may be more easily taken to heart and used in your daily life to bring you a greater sense of well being and health. Loving yourself is not the worst concept you ever tried to bring into your being. It may be the most important thing you ever did.

Here is a tool you could use to make loving yourself a reality. As I have worked with clients over the past twenty-some years, the exercise I have given out the most to people is something from Louise Hay's book *You Can Change Your Life*. It is an affirmation that really *could* change your life, and one that may positively assist you on your path. If you choose to do it, it is quite simple, but not easy.

Every day, twice a day, look in the mirror into your own eyes and say the words "I, *your full name here*, love, accept and appreciate myself exactly as I am" for several minutes. You may feel different emotions come up as you do this, for example, resistance, pain, fear, or guilt. Accept all of them, just noticing them without judging them. If you want to, you could keep a journal of all the emotions that come up and see how they change over time, or work with the emotions alone or with someone else at a later time (not during the exercise). Do this every day until you believe this statement completely. It may take a long time to feel that this is a true statement in every cell of your being, but these could be the most worthwhile words you ever spoke to yourself. It could take six weeks or six months, or it could take a year or more, but when you really believe this you will feel and know that it is true. It would be VERY unlikely that you would ever lose this belief again, but it's still a good practice to tell yourself regularly that you do indeed love yourself.

Self-Care

Self-care is another important area to acknowledge if you are to assist yourself on your quest for better general health and well-being. Self-care can sometimes get lost in the category of "I better not focus on what I need or it means I'm selfish," or in the category of "I'm too busy to do anything for myself," or "I don't deserve to do nice things for myself." All of these reasons need to be brought to conscious awareness and re-evaluated. Doing what you need to do to stay happy and sane is not selfish. You do deserve nice things in your life that bring you joy and balance and that help you become centered. And if you feel too busy, then you may choose a way to change your schedule that accommodates your self-care so that you can keep doing all those things better with more creativity, desire and effectiveness. If you are not the best at self-care now, remember that it is a possible choice, and only you can make it happen. Even if you have a family and many responsibilities it is possible to do something for yourself each day, if only for a few minutes. Doing so will also teach your children what it is and how to do it so they can create some healthy self-care practices for themselves. Hopefully you can take some larger portions of time on other days for yourself so that you can stay happy and keep functioning at your optimum and in good health.

Partial List of Self-Care Options

We all have preferences, likes and dislikes that relate to this area. Use this list to explore possible options for giving yourself the care and loving activities that you would like more of in your life. See what resonates with who you are and pass over what does not please or excite you.

1) Relaxing (whatever that means to you), basically doing nothing with a specific goal or agenda

2) Taking a hot bath with candlelight and music

3) Reading a good book

4) Writing in a journal

5) Listening to music, or creating your own music

6) Going for a walk, bike ride, run, swim, etc.

7) Doing a project that you enjoy (i.e. scrapbooking, photography, collecting of some kind)

8) Going out into nature for the sake of enjoying it

9) Praying or telling yourself positive messages

10) Getting a massage or other body work

11) Sitting still in quiet meditation

12) Being with friends

13) Interacting with a pet or watching outdoor animals such as birds

14) Joining a women's group or men's group of some kind, or a book club

15) Playing (games, sports, creative arts, music, whatever play is to you)

16) Laughing

17) Somehow coming into the present and back to your center, collecting yourself

18) Doing things you love, like going to concerts or other events, gardening, cooking, being with special people, seeing movies, etc.

19) Processing emotions with loved ones or in therapy

20) Moving your body through exercise or dance or anything that you enjoy

21) Creating something through an art form

22) Having dinner with someone you love or another kind of date

23) Hanging out with someone with no plans, just being and enjoying

24) Going on vacations or personal retreats

There are endless possibilities for nurturing your deepest needs and desires, so use your creativity to find your own ideas to feed yourself. If you can spend some time *each* day incorporating one or more of these ideas into your life or bringing joy to yourself, you will be a happier, healthier person. This can be much easier than it sounds.

Looking out my window right now at the large, beautiful snowflakes falling down is bringing me joy. The fallen snow painting the trees is lovely, and the little purple and yellow finches pecking away at the hanging birdfeeders makes me smile. They come in groups and eat together, then leave in groups, making way for the small woodpeckers to have their turn. Watching animal behavior is usually interesting and delightful to me. It helps me feel lighter.

It is what we notice, what we register as pleasing to us, not what is really around us, that matters. If you focus your internal lens to see something that will give you joy, you will probably not have to look very far. As you do this more and more, simple things will appear and bring you moments of joy more often. What you see and tell yourself, you will become. Loving yourself and your life will become easier if you allow yourself to see the beauty and to be grateful for all that is. Recently I was sitting at a table with three people when one of them said, "Do you ever find yourself thinking, I'm so glad to be alive?" We had a short conversation about this, and two of three people at the table said they often think that. If all of us had that as a regular thought, can you imagine how our world could change?

"There are two ways to live your life. One is as though nothing is a miracle. The other is as though everything is a miracle."
— *Albert Einstein*

Chapter 10

Solutions for a Healthier Lifestyle:
Spiritual Life

Spirit

There are so many spiritual aspects to life that many of us don't think about or see how they fit into the category of spirit. I am not talking about religion directly in this chapter, although for many, their spiritual life has a large religious element to it. Whether you find spiritual healing through religion or in other ways is nobody's business but your own. We each have our own set of life experiences that have brought us thus far on our spiritual journeys, and I believe that this is certainly an area that continues to deepen as we age. We all have our own path, and our spirituality is indeed a source of connection that is deeply personal. In my opinion, deepening the ways that we are spiritually connected to ourselves, to others, to community and to the earth and natural life around us, is a large part of spirituality. It is through faith that we learn how to deepen these aspects. Some of the things I mention here may seem more religious to you than others, but I am not advocating any particular kind of religion. In my eyes religions are more similar than they are different. My spirituality is one of inclusion.

The heart of spirituality for me is my faith, which becomes stronger within me every time that I connect with my own essence of divinity, the Godlike part of my nature, the gift that I came here to give the planet. It is in this place that I learn to trust myself and the world around me, having the knowledge that no matter what happens, I am able to handle it through my faith. It is my belief that we have all come here with our own divine purpose(s) to share with the world. When we are unclear about what that purpose is, there may be a disconnection between and among our physical, mental, and spiritual bodies. The spirit part of us always knows our purpose, but sometimes we get lost and off our path and that information is forgotten and unknown to our mind and mental processes. The quest for remembering our purpose is certainly a spiritual journey all its own.

So how do we get re-connected to this part of ourselves? This has become more and more difficult for many of us as we have become so busy with "life" that we lose our alone time and the quietness that connects us to our divine self. The speed with which we move through our day has become dizzying to most everyone I know, including myself. What we really need to do to connect with ourselves is to slow down, literally stop moving, to FEEL OURSELF in our surroundings and just "be." This is where our connection to our spiritual nature can be found. It is in the stillness, the place of emptiness where the answers lie, where we can reconnect or find the space to remember what it is we came here to do. When it is noisy internally or externally we may lose our way.

Many of us find that through meditation, contemplation, or quiet solitude we find the answers to our deepest questions in life, like "who am I?", and "what am I here to do with my life?", as well as "how do I learn what is true for me?" and "how can I feel safe in a world that is changing so quickly?" Being quiet and reflecting can help us to process our difficult emotions and experiences or to just let them be as they are and accept what is. It is also in these quiet moments that we just feel ourself, a human being on this planet, one of billions, and yet unique. To sit quietly with yourself may not be easy. And that in itself is important information to realize. Why is it not easy? For some it is their mind that can't be quiet, for others it is their body that brings distractions. Not many people can sit quietly and comfortably with themselves for a period of time, *unless they have practiced doing it.* Many of us spend our lives distracting ourselves from what's going on inside, and sometimes when we actually do sit quietly, it can be painful.

Why is this? Are we afraid of what we might feel? Or notice? Or come to understand? If we are generally disconnected from our essence and our divinity, then we may experience some kind of negative feelings around the process of sitting quietly. Even if we're not disconnected that can be so, but I have a hunch it is more difficult for those who are afraid of what they may find there in the pseudo silence. (I say this because the mind is always thinking and moving and is not by nature quiet.) If we realize that it is from this place of sitting and listening and not judging ourselves that we have more connection to our spirit, then we are more likely to experiment with it. Like so many other things in life, it is through practice that we become comfortable with just being, and that we actually notice how it benefits our daily lives to just sit in quiet solitude, or even to just stand and breathe and become centered in a brief moment while we're waiting in line, or in the restroom. If we all would breathe and become centered several times a day and FEEL ourselves, I believe our world would be a different place. Being connected to the spiritual part of ourselves can happen at any moment really, it just takes the conscious awareness of being IN that moment, noticing what is happening without attaching to it or deciding anything about it other than "this is what is happening." I often think that the reason we love our vacations so much is that we can finally stop all the busyness and just enjoy the moments, fully taking them in, and leave behind all the mind chatter and the constant "doing." Allowing joy to surface, feeling a deep sense of relaxation and connection with one's self and those around us is very satisfying and ultimately a spiritual experience. It lets you see yourself as you are, while not in a human DOING state, rather a human BEING state. It also brings about true connection with other people, which for most people is what life is all about.

So I encourage you to sit quietly, learn meditation, find a spiritual path that leads you to your divinity, and be with it regularly. The feeling of connecting with one's self can be different for each of us. For some it may bring elation or a sense of deep peace. For others it may feel like pure relaxation or deep satisfaction as if all is right in that moment. Some people have amazing revelations or remember what they are here for, giving them a renewing lift of their spirit. Hopefully your spiritual path will bring you to an emotional place that helps you feel full and balanced and loved. For some people this may come by taking a walk in the woods, for some it may be writing in a journal, and for others it may be meditating or even exercising. I have done all of these things and I can say that each brings a different quality of connection to self. Personally, it is in sitting in meditation that I receive the most benefit in connecting with my deepest self. But on some days what I need most is to move my body to better connect with it and get my energy flowing, and a walk out in nature is exactly what I need at that moment. There is not one silver bullet, and you also may have several different ways to deeply connect with yourself, using them at different times. Experimenting and being flexible with where you are at in the moment will bring you the deepest healing of your spirit, and of your body and mind.

Faith

What is faith? Faith has to do with confidence or a belief or trust in something or someone beyond oneself. Some say it is an unquestioning belief that does not require proof or evidence. Other definitions in the dictionary include "complete trust, confidence, or reliance; an unquestioning belief in God, religious tenets, etc; an allegiance to some person or thing; loyalty; or a belief in something that is unseen."

What is it to be faithful? To be faithful means keeping faith; maintaining allegiance to someone or something; or it implies a continued steadfast adherence to a person or thing to which one is bound by an oath, duty, or obligation. I don't think faith necessarily has to do with religion. For some it is certainly linked to a religion, while many others have a deep faith that is not linked to religion. This makes it all the more intriguing because it shows that faith can be developed through a wide-ranging number of paths. Faith is personal, though it can have a public dimension to it, as when people pray together. Some would say that faith is about the relationship they have with God or a higher power. My focus here is on the personal dimension of faith. Though faith is unique to each of us, I think the nature of it, or practice of it is meant to encourage each of us to strive toward what is positive or what leads to wholeness in this existence we call life. Faith for me is believing in a set of spiritual truths which have been shown to me through my experiences, and which continue to expand as I mature.

Because we live our lives in a constant flow of ever-changing experiences, never one day the same as the last, always moving to what is next, faith can be tricky. Then we add the fact that our internal nature is also in a constant pattern of movement, with emotions, thoughts and new things happening every second inside of us, as well as around us. One can see how it becomes even more necessary and yet difficult to have or keep a deep sense of faith.

It may be easier to maintain faith when our children are healthy, when we have employment that feeds the family, when we have a place to live. But these are not necessarily the times when we need faith the most. It is when illness comes, when we lose the job, when we become homeless, when there is an accident; this is when faith in a power beyond ourselves can be most useful. This is when we are called upon to remember and practice our deepest faith. Sometimes life's difficulties can inspire us to search for answers related to faith, or can help us deepen into what we already hold as true. Once we have this deep connection with a sustaining faith, it may be very hard to lose that faith, hopefully for the rest of our lives. But as nothing is permanent, one's faith can also become rattled and even given up on, or lost for periods of time.

I have a friend who lost her only son by way of a horrible murder. From that day on, her faith was changed forever, and it probably still continues to move and change, to disintegrate and to come back together in new directions as the many years pass since her son's death. The same is the case when you think about children who lose their parent to an illness that cannot be stopped, or an accident that changes one's life forever. In these cases, the faith that we build our lives around is completely altered, sometimes crushed forever, sometimes lost for just a while, until a new and different relationship or understanding of faith makes sense. I know people that have completely given up on faith, and I know more who come to experience love and faith through hard circumstances. In this process their belief in the goodness of people, and/or a loving God or spirit is stronger than their grief.

My faith strengthens me when I need it, it helps me to get through the difficult times and keeps me focused on the potential in myself and the world around me as I continue to believe in a positive universal force that guides our lives. Maybe the basis of having faith is centered on believing that love is, or "should" (I don't generally like to use this word but it fits here) be the primary inspiration of human beings. Maybe not having true faith is what happens when fear is the primary inspiration of human beings. Of course when this is the case, it is an unconscious force that guides us rather than what we think of as a choice we've made. Most people would not aspire to be guided by fear, and yet, when they look honestly at what helps them make decisions or even form opinions about things, they may find that fear IS their driving force in many cases. Fear unfortunately restricts our choices as we make decisions. It tends to bring us into resisting what is present, or into denying what is there because it is too painful for us to actually see the truth. In either case, we become tight or contracted internally and unable to connect with our inner wisdom or our divinity. If fear becomes a pattern for us, we may at some point also form a pattern of feeling isolated, depressed and shut down. It is hard to feel faith or love from this perspective.

Whether your beliefs lean toward love or fear would certainly change your perception of the world around you. I bring this idea forth because it is an extremely valuable question to ask yourself if you lean toward fear or love when making decisions or choosing your behaviors. Most of us have probably not looked at this idea in this way or asked ourselves directly how we operate. Yet the answer shapes our values, behaviors and attitudes in everyday living, and knowing which perspective we're coming from can ultimately give us some information about our own faith. Fear blocks us, while love helps us see the possibilities and the ways in which we are connected to something larger than ourselves. With love we can see or imagine what potential and capabilities we have, and our faith brings us closer to actualizing them. With love we can also look at the depths of suffering that we see around us and bring compassion to all of the pain we see, with an understanding that people are more similar than different and all pain is pain, and all love is love. We all want to be free of suffering.

Faith and love are forces that can motivate people toward something positive. Fear can also motivate us, but not necessarily in the direction we might consciously choose to go. For instance, some people are overly concerned with having power or having security, and it may drive them to do things they aren't proud of or wouldn't do if they were not pushed by their fear of not having either power or security.

For example, someone might stay in a job that is not at all satisfying to them, or one that is even harmful to their health because they want security above all else. When we act out of fear we become limited in our responses to life. When we don't notice this happening, it can easily become detrimental to us and those around us. Some people are consciously working toward releasing their fear(s) as they realize how fear can distort their reality. These people have realized that they are blocking their own creativity and being held back by their fear-based distortions of reality. It is freeing and empowering to make choices based on love and the common good. I believe we need to have a basic sense of goodwill toward ourselves and others to hold our deepest possible faith. We need to know that as human beings we are imperfect, and yet we continue to strive to become a better person and to do good things in the world.

Remembering that life happens with or without us, and that we can't always control it, can actually be of comfort. Yes, we can decide to choose consciously how to respond to the difficulties that we are faced with. But ultimately the outcome will be what it is, after we do our best, and from there we get to choose again how well we accept what comes to pass. Faith helps us here. We do our part, and then we let go. And if things are not turning out the way we want them to, well, that is how life goes sometimes. It's better to be realistic about this fact than to fight against something that cannot change in the manner you wish it would. Even a very tenacious person needs to realize, through faith, when it is best to surrender and move on. Acceptance, compassion, gratitude and love will help us when moving on is the next step in our faith journey.

With faith, we can find a way to step forward into the unknown, as we have done over and over again, and become confident that no matter what happens we will get through this too, one way or another.

Questions about Faith

1) What does faith mean to you?

2) Do you have a religious tradition or faith that you feel was given to you by a parent or a church?

3) If so, does it fully fit with who you have become now? In what ways yes or no?

4) In what areas of your life does fear guide or motivate you?

5) In what areas of your life does love guide or motivate you?

6) Can you see how fear may be restricting you, and would you like to become more free and empowered in those areas?

7) Do you believe that people are basically good or basically bad (or evil)?

8) Can you see how this last question may be related to your tendency toward love or fear?

9) Do you feel motivated by a positive force you call faith?

10) How might faith contribute to changing fear into love?

11) How might strengthening your faith move you in a more positive direction?

Spiritual Practices

Having a regular spiritual practice is extremely important for living a balanced life. For some people this may have to do with a church community, but even if that is one way you connect to spirit, I think it is also important to have a spiritual practice that you do alone. I will mention some ideas for you here, and of course, there are many more. Praying or meditating can be spiritual practices. Doing yoga can be a spiritual practice, depending on the type of yoga and the teacher's way of teaching. Doing Chi Gung or Tai Chi are spiritual practices, and so can walking, mowing the lawn, or cleaning be. Creating a painting or any other art form could be a spiritual practice for you. It is in your intention that the mundane things can become spiritual experiences. What I mean is if you go out on a walk to empty your busy mind and become connected to your essence again, it will be a spiritual practice. If you go out on a walk with a device in your ears talking at you or singing at you, or talking with a friend, it may not connect you with your deep center. So setting the intention of doing something with the purpose of clearing yourself of all the information and energies that distract you will likely be much more useful in reconnecting you to your spiritual essence. Of course this doesn't mean there's anything wrong with going for a walk with a friend, on the contrary; it's just that if your intention is to connect with your divinity, it would be a more reachable goal if you did something alone. You can also deeply connect with yourself while in a group of people doing certain kinds of yoga or Tai Chi or meditating, or being in a purposefully spiritual setting could also bring you to your divine essence.

Our challenge in connecting with the spiritual parts of ourselves lies in the busyness of our culture. Because most of us are receiving huge amounts of stimulation throughout the day just through the act of living, we need to clear out our minds regularly to find our spiritual center. This is reason enough for each of us to sit quietly for a time each day doing absolutely nothing (even for five minutes) so that we can allow our nervous system to have complete rest. Doing just that would positively affect our overall health, and in the space and the quiet is where we can connect with our spirit. Optimally we would be able to spend more quiet time alone on a regular basis to deepen our relationship to spirit. But in this fast-paced life many of us lead, even a short time is better than none. Our priorities will dictate the actual time spent on our spiritual relationship.

It is my hope that the items I have listed above will open you up to the many possibilities for deepening your own spiritual practice. These are yours to discover and to enjoy. I think you will find the search and the practice completely worthwhile as you feel yourself living more and more from this spiritual center and in deep connection with your soul. The following chapters offer other ideas for enriching your spiritual practices. Excellent reading on the topic of spirit or soul can also be found in the relatively new book by Deepak Chopra called *Reinventing the Body, Resurrecting the Soul.*

"I go to nature to be soothed and healed and to have my senses put in order."
— *John Burrows*

Spiritual Moments

There are many opportunities in our human life to receive the gift of spirit. I regularly have these experiences, partly because I am sensitive and aware of them and have become open to receiving them. It may take an awareness of the details around you to feel and see a spiritual gift. And it may also take the gift of being in the moment to appreciate the little things that can touch you so deeply.

One gift I have received from my mother is true appreciation of the beauty in the natural world around me. It might be in the form of a colorful flower, or a tiny butterfly, or a bird singing their happy song, but I receive so much joy from paying attention to nature. It brings me back to a childlike part of myself, where the simplest things can really be nourishing. Most often it is in the small things that I delight, but of course, an incredible mountain or river touches me very deeply, and sustains my belief in God or something bigger than myself. These times I cherish, and I need them regularly to continue happily on my journey. Living in a city, I need to get out of it as often as possible to go to the quiet places in nature that feed me. It may take hours or longer periods of time to bring myself fully back as a nourished being who can then give to and help nourish others.

When I was 30 years old, I was going through a difficult time physically with ovarian problems and became completely drained on all levels. From everything I've learned, I think I had chronic fatigue syndrome, though I never got a doctor's diagnosis. What I needed was a huge change, and a long rest. I moved to Sedona, Arizona after having spent five incredible days there on a vacation months before. If you have ever been to Sedona, you will probably know what drew me there. It is a place of amazing natural beauty surrounded by red rock mountain formations, lots of green trees and a beautiful flowing creek. It is a perfect place for healing. I went there to find my strength, my center, my new direction in life, and to reconnect with my spiritual being, which had been short of attention in the life I was living.

I rented a very small trailer home, forty feet from Oak Creek, which for a Midwesterner like me should really be called a river because of its width and wild rapids that flow in many places along it, including right in front of my trailer. This home was the smallest place I've ever lived in, and my favorite home to date. I was in the woods, on the river, between two mountains, and all around me I was bathed in a beauty like no other I had ever experienced. This was the perfect place for me at that time to become quiet, to go within, and to connect with nature and my own spiritual essence that I had been too busy to attend to. I still feel a very deep spiritual connection to Sedona and its land, and yearn for it. From living there, I became familiar with many of the beautiful hikes and areas that most tourists don't get to experience, but I had learned about them from the locals who became my friends. The heights to which I experienced my deep connection to the earth, to the people, and to the spirit that lives in me and completely surrounds me always, will never be lost in my memory. I can and do go to Sedona in my mind when I need to find my way back to my self. Sedona has become "my happy place." I can usually just visualize being there and it gives me a strong feeling and sense of self that I can always call up if and when I need to.

If you have had one or more of these kinds of experiences in your life, you may wish to solidify the memory and use it in meditation or other times to help yourself remember who you are when you are completely connected to yourself and to the world around you. This is one of the gifts you can give to yourself over and over again.

Beauty

Seeing beauty and resonating with it, really enjoying it and feeling it in your body, is a healing practice all its own. We are beautiful beings, and when we see beauty it reminds us of our higher selves. Some people have never realized this, and they lose out on so much. They not only forget to appreciate the beauty in themselves, but they don't allow themselves to experience the beauty around them. Bringing more beauty into your life is another spiritual practice. It creates a space from which you can appreciate and be grateful for what you have and that brings you more love, acceptance and a general sense of well-being. In the world we live in, noticing and feeling beauty is one of the simplest ways that we can open our hearts. It is important for our health that we open our hearts regularly. So never underestimate the power of beauty, in whatever form. It is everywhere: In music, in art, in color, in plants, flowers, trees, all of nature, in your children and your lover, in people you pass on the street, in a pet, or in a stranger's smile. One simple red rose could bring you beauty and joy for a week. Noticing and enjoying these small but omnipresent examples of beauty in your life can lift your spirit to help you feel lighter during hard times or any time. Find your own ways for seeing and feeling beauty throughout your whole being. Write these things down and see how easy it is to surround yourself with those things that give you a smile. It is that short break in the present moment and the act of refocusing that can bring you back to knowing that everything is going to be all right (and sometimes to keep you from taking yourself too seriously).

Prayer

What is prayer? It seems to be different from one person to the next. My type of prayer is probably not the same as yours, but as long as prayer is something that brings you into connection with what is holy to you, it doesn't matter how it is done. For me, that is a connection to all that is, to God, to the Great Spirit, and to the holy in and around me. I pray out loud and nonverbally, and I believe that both make a difference. I pray before doing energy work on my clients as a way to set the space for the intention of the healing and for all that happens to be in their highest good. I pray at dinner with my family. I sometimes pray at night before bed. I pray when I need help with something in my life. Whenever I pray, I feel heard. It didn't used to be that way for me though. I grew up in a family that never prayed. My parents became Unitarian when I was very young and they don't really believe in God, so they never prayed in front of me as a child. I went to Catholic churches as a child with my friends, and heard prayer there. My mind and body had some strange feelings during some of the prayers, and I decided that prayer was not really for me. I wish now that someone had talked with me about prayer as a child, given me a larger perspective, or told me what it meant to them or how I could use it.

It wasn't until I began my training for Hands-on-Healing that I really heard prayers that meant something to me. I found out that I am very connected to Native American spirituality, and that things of nature and of the earth are easy for me to pray to. At meals I used to thank all the animals that gave up their lives so that I could be nourished by them, and sometimes I still do. I loved learning about the four directions (of Native Americans) and what each one meant and the gifts they each give to us and how to pray for them. Over the years of becoming more comfortable with who I am spiritually, the more I have prayed, and the more prayer means to me. I have learned that what we say out loud especially, has an effect on the beings around us, and therefore words need to be carefully chosen, especially in prayer. What we say matters, because we put an energy out in the world that gets picked up somewhere. If I send a prayer to Iraq or Afghanistan I believe that that energy is noticed and added to the other prayers for peace being sent to Iraq (or any country in war or turmoil). This is how we collectively change the energy of something that has been in a negative pattern. There has even been research done that shows that when others pray for someone's healing it has a positive effect on their ability to heal. (Read, for example, about the double-blind study done by Larry Dossey as described in the book *Healing Words.*)

So even if you are uncomfortable with prayer today, it may one day become a tool for your own healing. If you are the least bit curious about it, give it a try, alone or with others. You may be surprised at how it can make you feel lighter, more peaceful or give you more clarity regarding the issues in your life. Just speaking the words can relieve you, allow you to let things go, and remind you that this too shall pass and that your life matters.

Angels, Guides and Helpers

Have you ever had the feeling of being held somehow, or being saved from a brush with danger unexpectedly? Once when I was driving on the highway in a huge downpour of rain, I couldn't see all of a sudden, not even to pull over to the side of the road. I prayed to my guardian angel, and all at once I was there on the side of the road, parked and safe. I don't know how it happened, but it did. I was so grateful for the miracle, and felt I was not alone. Interestingly in this instance I was traveling home after seeing a woman who was dying, and we'd had a beautiful connection. It was the last time I would see her alive, and I think I was very near to the spirit world that day, so having an angel with me seemed perfectly right.

Through personal experiences like these over the years, and as I gained my belief in God or a Divine Source, I have also come to believe in the existence of angels, guides and helpers. But it took me a while to come to that belief. If you are not someone who has personally had any experience with the angelic realm or you have not heard of others' experiences with it, this may be a difficult idea. Questioning something unknown to you is healthy. It may also be useful to be curious and to consider being open to the possibility that these helpers exist. Being open to the presence of angels or fully believing in them has brought a more humane and joyous life experience to many people. You really have nothing to lose and only something to gain by running your own experiments on the matter.

Angels are said to be spiritual beings, often depicted as messengers of God in the Hebrew and Christian Bibles, as well as in the Quran. The English word "angel" comes from the Greek word *angelos* which means "messenger." Some believe that an angel is a pure spirit created by God. Angels were common in ancient Greek philosophy and were alluded to by Plato in Phaedo, 108.

There are endless spiritual icons with multiple names in many different traditions. In addition to several types of angels, many believe there are saints, ascended masters, gods, goddesses, deities, and animal totems to be included as spiritual icons. Working with these helpers/beings is another resource for us in this life that is not always easy to navigate. So many people feel alone in the world, and having more ways to gain support and enrich our spiritual lives is helpful. If you would like to explore this possibility, there are several books by Doreen Virtue, PhD who has written extensively on this subject.

The presence of angels and spiritual deities really became apparent to me through my work as a healer. Years ago I was discussing the topic of energy work with another healer, and she suggested that I could ask for and receive help from a spiritual entity whenever I needed it. I was skeptical, but she insisted that she had been doing it for years and that I should just try it to see what would happen. So one day when I was doing energy work with a client, I felt that I needed help. I internally called on Jesus of Nazareth to bring his healing hands in to work with mine. I immediately received a jolt of energy that shifted the energy that had been present in the room moments before. This was a little eerie to me, I must say, and yet I tried this several more times, with several more clients, and each time, I felt the same jolt of energy come in as my body would actually feel a shiver go through it. I would then feel a stronger flow of energy coming through me and into my client, and sometimes get messages about what to do next in the healing session.

Some years later, one of my clients who was clairvoyant (she has the gift of seeing things that others don't usually see) asked me after several sessions of working together if I knew that I had two healing angels that regularly work with me. I asked her what they looked like. She told me the two colors in which she saw them and other details. They happen to be my two favorite colors. Other clients have reported feeling like there were still hands on places on their body that I had been holding, even after I had moved on to another place. I wonder if my healing angels were continuing with the work? After a time, I surrendered to believing that I am not alone in my work, and that if I ask for help, I will receive it. I now ask for help on any occasion, not just when I am working.

People have told me over the years of several instances in which they feel sure that an angelic presence kept them from harm or death. Two men I knew fell from heights two and three stories up, one landing on pavement. Both walked away from these incidents feeling as though they were guided gently down by some strange force. Sometimes the stories are about a person who was supposed to be on a certain plane, or in a subway or car that ended up crashing, but for some odd reason they never made the trip. I've heard stories from parents whose children have seen angels, and I wonder if we all could see them if we had not been told that this was preposterous. Children often have very interesting and wise words to say about angels or God if you ask them. I believe that children are still close enough to the spirit world to know (or remember) a bit more than many adults do about these topics.

I attribute the most incredible miracle of survival in my family circle to the presence of angels when my niece Freda was in a motorcycle crash. She was a passenger on a motorcycle driven by a young man who was traveling at a very high speed when her body was thrown off the motorcycle. She received serious injuries on three sides of her body, so it appears she rolled. I feel sure that she was protected by her angels who wrapped her up so to speak, as best they could. There were so many ways that she could have died in this accident, but she lived. I believe her angels knew it was not her time to go. I will go more deeply into this healing story in the next chapter.

Susan Gregg wrote the book *The Encyclopedia of Angels, Spirit Guides and Ascended Masters.* She believes that helpers are always there but they wish to be invited in rather than imposing on you. If you ask and accept their aid, they will be there, but they will always respect your free will except in the case of saving one's life, when they may take over. The only way to really find out if you have angels, guides and helpers who work with you is to test it out, to experiment and see what happens. Your angels can be another way to access your connection to your spirit. They can help to deepen your sense of faith and even your belief in yourself.

If you choose to experiment with this potential relationship you could have with these guides, start small. You may want to ask for help in finding a parking spot, or ask for guidance on a pressing matter that is on your mind, and then remain open to receiving an answer. These are the ways to gain the experiences that may dissolve your doubt over time. Then go on to call on your guardian angel when you're feeling afraid or when you are in trouble. Or try asking your healing angels to work with you when you are sick. This has helped me when I was battling something small like a headache or bellyache, or something more difficult like walking pneumonia.

Trusting that there is help for us can be the hardest part. We are often taught not to ask for help and instead, some people are told they are deficient if they don't do everything on their own. So just asking for help can be a growing experience for us, not to mention the trust that builds if we begin to receive the help. We might also hold the belief that we don't deserve the help. Of course we do! We all deserve help, love and kindness. There is no reason we need to move through difficult times without help and support when it is available to us. I am clear that suffering is NOT the reason we are here. Even those who are not Christian can find some wisdom in the saying of Jesus, "Ask and you shall receive."

Questions around your spiritual life and practices

1) Do you presently take time out of your day to connect in some way with what you would call your spirit?

2) Do you have a belief or understanding of what your spirit or soul is?

3) Do you feel that your faith is strong, or do you even know what that might look like?

4) Do you feel that having some quiet time for yourself each day would be useful for connecting with the deeper and more spiritual part of yourself?

5) Would you like to create a spiritual practice to bring yourself more in touch with the divine part of yourself?

6) Would you like to learn more about spirituality and faith?

7) Have you ever tried meditation?

8) Do you know that it is not typically easy for any of us to sit quietly and just "be"? (And yet we do it anyway because of the benefits we gain from this practice.)

9) Are there places you have been to that have connected you to your deepest essence?

10) Can you see and feel beauty outside of you that warms and touches you deeply?

11) Can you appreciate yourself and the gifts that you bring to this world?

12) Can you trust yourself and awaken to the truth within you?

Another way of connecting with these spirit guides is to go into meditation and after focusing on your breath for a short time, you can call in a certain deity whom you would like to work with. Then be open and listen, see or sense whatever is there for you in the exchange. Or you can create a simple but sacred ritual to get in touch with these helpers. This might be lighting a candle or saying a prayer or creating a sacred space in your home in which you regularly go to connect with these angels, saints and deities. They may bring you very useful information about something in particular, or teach you more about the spiritual aspects of yourself. Allow a relationship to develop in whatever way feels right for you. These wise beings are here for those who wish to seek their celestial love and guidance.

Gratitude

In many spiritual traditions there is an emphasis on gratitude. This is another tool we can use that slows us down, brings us back to our center and to what is important, and allows our perspective to expand. There is a big world out there, and sometimes we get so wrapped up in the dramas and details of the day that we forget the big picture, and the many gifts that are present in our lives all of the time.

If you are an American who can read, right there you have a lot to be thankful for. We have so much available to us here, that people in other countries cannot even fathom our lifestyles or the endless opportunities we have. We are a wealthy country, and though not all of us have wealth, it is true that we have more than many other countries in the world. We, at the very least, have drinkable and running water and plumbing, which people in some places cannot say. Traveling to other countries is always a great way to realize just how much we have to be grateful for. We tend to downplay the basic amenities in our life that are not available to others, like all the water we want to use, or enough heat in our home, or the ability to drive to work every day. (I realize that some Americans don't have these things, but the vast majority does.) Most children here do not have to suffer in the ways that many other children throughout the world suffer every day. And we do not live with war in our land and the constant trauma arising from this painful state of conflict.

It is really quite easy to sit down and write a list of the many things that you are grateful for, and I recommend it. This is a spiritual practice that will expand your gratitude and open you more fully to the gifts that you live with daily. Realizing this and being regularly conscious about your many blessings will likely change the way you view your life, yourself, and the world. Feeling gratitude brings more gratitude and experiencing that can very often bring more that is good into your life, or maybe it just accentuates your awareness of the gratitude. Either way, it feels good and it spreads goodness. "What goes around, comes around" as they say.

What I am about to say, I feel is closely related to gratitude. When a person can open his or herself up to feeling deeply moved on a regular basis, it is to me a sign of being close to your spirit or soul. For instance, to look into a baby's eyes and tear up because of the beauty you see there, or the pure perfection you see in them, this is a spiritual moment. It is you connecting to the pure spirit of that child with your own spirit. Meeting someone who has been through real hardship and come out the other side may be another of these occasions to feel deeply moved by their strong spirit and resolve to make their life better. Or sometimes just in conversation with another we are moved to happy tears, or sad tears, while really listening to them and feeling their depths in the words that we hear. I am often deeply touched by movies, especially true stories of those who have struggled and triumphed. To be able to feel in this way is a gift of connecting to one's spirit and feeling gratitude for the moment. It is often simple like looking at a flower or animal, noticing the sunset, or seeing a beautiful, large tree spreading its lovely branches out to touch us quietly. There are so many times in my life when I feel I am connected to the "One," and to the deep place in me where I know I fit in and belong to this world.

"Each dawn brings life's precious gift; another day in which to live, to love and to find happiness."

— *Unknown*

Chapter 11

Freda's Story

The most incredible healing experience I've been a part of in my life as a healer has been with my niece, Freda. It was by far the most difficult for me, and the most rewarding, and it moved me to a depth I have no words for.

Freda, a strong and fit 15-year old girl, was on a motorcycle outside of Lanesboro, Minnesota when she and the driver of the bike crashed going around a curve. They both hit their heads on rocks, and neither of them had a helmet on. Her companion died at the scene and Freda had several serious injuries. Her skull was crushed by a rock that penetrated her brain about two inches deep and about as big around as a tennis ball, leaving her with a traumatic brain injury. We found out later that this part of her brain corresponded to her right motor function. She also had a severely broken jaw that was in three pieces, with a bone sticking out under her chin/neck area. She had a break in the part of her skull that was all of one half inch from her brain stem, and ten broken or cracked vertebrae from T2-T11.

Each one of these injuries was devastating, and yet she miraculously did not sever her spinal chord. At the time of the accident her doctors and family had no idea what this would result in for Freda. She was kept in an induced coma over the next few days so that her brain could be less active during the surgeries and healing that took place. This also made the waiting and wondering more difficult, because she couldn't have woken up even if she tried to. You can imagine how incredibly difficult this was for our whole family.

Freda was at the Mayo Clinic (who did a great job with her) and I did not go to see her until a few days after the accident because she was in surgeries for three days in a row for her brain, jaw and back. There were plenty of support people there but I wanted to wait until I could get my hands on her, literally. I had been doing this healing work for years, and specifically on people after surgeries to accelerate their healing. I was so pleased that I could use it on Freda. I was ready and very happy that I could actually DO something.

Because two of Freda's surgeries were eight and nine hours each, she was full of anesthesia and the first thing I do after someone's surgery is to clear their energy field of the drugs. Let me quickly define an energy field so that you will know what I'm talking about. It will also be more clearly defined in another chapter. Our energy field, sometimes called auric field or biofield, is an area around our body that is a part of us in that it relates to our physical, emotional, mental and spiritual consciousness. All of these parts in turn, CAN and DO influence our physical body constantly. Most of us have had the experience of someone coming too close to us in a public place, and we feel like they just got in our space. They actually did touch a part of us, even though it wasn't our physical body; it was our energy field, but we could feel them just the same. Working on someone through their energy field will change the field, and the purpose is to clear, strengthen and balance the field which will in turn affect the body.

Freda's energy field at this point was different than anyone's I had ever felt before. I can feel a person's energy field as I run my hands about four inches over their body. There is a sensation in my hand that varies due to what is going on in that person's body. Because of Freda's neurological and spinal issues, her nervous system was totally distressed. I felt this as electricity in my fingertips, almost like an electrical burn. Her body was so overstimulated that all I could do for the first two treatments was to clear energy and trauma from her energy field. This clearing takes the anesthesia out of her energy field so that she had only the anesthesia left in her body to detoxify, allowing the body to get to the work of healing itself more quickly. The clearing of the field also helps to reconnect the damaged tissue and assist the body in returning to its normal flow of energy. When I tried to work on her head, the only thing her body could tolerate was clearing. (Bodies often give me messages as I'm working on them, and hers was loud and clear on many occasions about what it wanted or did not want.) Her body could not tolerate any energy added into her body until the third session, which was one week after her accident.

On that day, one of the most dramatic and exciting things happened after working on Freda. She was still unconscious, a week had passed, but she had been off of the coma-inducing medication for three days and we were all very nervous about when and if she would wake up. The doctors would not make a prediction, as brain injuries can be different every time, and nobody really knows what will happen. To me, as I felt her energy field on this eighth day, it now exhibited about half of the neurological overload as it had the other two days I had worked on her. I again did the energy field clearing and then began working on specific injured areas. I added some energy into her body through her feet this time, and she tolerated it. I did half of a chakra connection, bringing energy up to her hips, which was all she wanted. Then I was able to do what we call a brain balance, a technique that balances both hemispheres, but only for about two to three minutes before her body "kicked me off" so to speak. I could feel her body saying "that's all I can take in right now." She was done, and I drove back home to the Twin Cities.

About 90 minutes after I got home, Freda's father called, in tears, and said Freda had "woken up." She had tracked him with her eyes, while he was walking across the room for over a minute, and then responded to the nurse and the doctor when they gave her hand signals to repeat. Not only was she conscious, but she had some obvious brain function as she was able to respond to them. We were all ecstatic and crying with joy. I don't know for sure if the energy work was the cause of her becoming conscious, but the timing was interesting. It's very likely that it was not a complete coincidence.

I continued to work on Freda, about every five days or so initially, and then further apart. It was quite an emotional challenge for me to be there, but one I completely wanted to take on. Just seeing all of the machines she was hooked up to, especially at the beginning, was difficult, but it quickly forced me to desensitize myself to that and to move on with what I was there to do. That experience has made me quite comfortable in other hospital settings I've been in since because it was hard not only because of the "machines" but *especially* because it was my niece in the bed.

We had some interesting situations in the second and third weeks when she was getting quite feisty and moving around in her bed, trying to rewire her brain (the nurses told me). I had to hold her in the bed many times, and she was VERY strong and pushing against me. It was emotionally painful to see her suffering in physical pain and the frustration at not being able to talk. We had many extremely moving moments that I will never forget.

I worked on Freda about ten times in two and a half months. She healed very fast and more fully than expected, beating all timelines in the process. Initially, the doctors thought she would be walking in ten months or so, but she walked in one month. On that day one of the orthopedic surgeons who had put her broken back together came up to see her progress. When she walked across the room for him, he cried. It was a miracle and he knew it! Her struggle to find her way back to herself was not peaches and cream though; it was very hard work. She had speech, occupational and physical therapy every day, and they worked her hard. She had to learn everything over again that involved motor (movement) on the right side of her body and she was right handed, so that meant picking up her arm, feeding herself, everything. It all had to get rewired into a different part of her brain because where the memory had been was lost completely. Freda is a very strong young woman, and she wanted to do everything possible to get herself out of the hospital as soon as she could. Her attitude was stellar, and she had a lot of support from loved ones, especially from her mom who brought in humor in just the right moments, and her father who adores her. After three weeks in ICU and three weeks doing all of her therapies, she miraculously left the hospital on the summer solstice, only six weeks after her accident.

Part of the energy field clearing I did was to help clear the trauma and body memory of the accident out of her field before it became lodged in the density of the body. What is in the energy field can go into the body and what is in the body can go out into the energy field (I will expand on this idea in later chapters). Freda received this energy field clearing regularly during the first three weeks, when she has no memory of her hospital stay, which is truly a blessing. I believe it enabled her to heal more quickly and on many levels. In addition to her speedy physical recovery, she was seen by a psychiatrist only once. He said she was emotionally healthy enough to not see him again. From what I had heard about traumatic brain injury, the hard part can be the emotional and mental healing after the physical healing takes place. She has been unusually well-adjusted to the whole accident and its implications. I think this may be because the trauma that she might have had was cleared (or mostly cleared) before she ever had conscious awareness of it.

A month or so after Freda was home, I asked her what she had thought of her injury and her situation when she first woke up. I was referring to the time she was in rehab, about three weeks after the accident, and the point at which she has her first memories. She said she thought "I've had a bad accident, but I'm ok." Now that is a remarkable response! Many people would think, "Wow – am I messed up!" or "I'll never be the same." Or "Oh my God, now what do I do?" But her attitude was totally positive. Her personality is normally like that, AND I think that maybe her attitude was so positive because the body memory of her trauma was gone. What this allowed her to do was let her body heal the way an extremely fit 15-year-old would, if there was no interference from her mind.

When we have worries and fear, the body does not do as well at its job of healing. I have witnessed many people taking an extraordinarily long time to heal something because their mental and emotional faculties got in the way. I think in this case, Freda's mind and attitude was as remarkable as her physical healing.

Freda still had two more major surgeries to endure in the next six months after her accident. She had to have a plastic covering put in her head to cover the hole after all the swelling went down and enough healing of the tissue had taken place. She also had a complicated and painful jaw surgery a couple of months after that. In both cases, I went to Mayo to work on her immediately following her surgeries, and in both cases she had an afternoon surgery and went home the following morning, which was remarkable. Even the doctors thought so. She responded very well to the energy work, and as you can imagine, she was delighted to get out of the hospital!

Freda's physical, speech and occupational therapies continued throughout the rest of that summer. In the fall, four months after her accident, she started her sophomore year in school full time. She did better at school that year than she had ever done before; her parents say she finally applied herself. She says she's gained wisdom she never had before and realized that she has been given a second chance at life, so she's going to be a little more serious about her future. She spent her senior year of high school at the International School in Brussels, Belgium due to her older sister living there. She is now in her junior year in college at Purdue University and loves it! Freda can run, which is one of her passions, even with titanium rods in her back. She isn't in a lot of pain, and she still never complains. She still has a great attitude and is one of the most loving people I know.

For me, working with her was an incredibly difficult and beautiful experience. It expanded me in many ways and made me a better healer. I have a deep love for her, and still want to touch her every time I see her. Our connection is an example of one of the most wonderful aspects of my work. Though my emotions have run deeper than usual in this situation, I have a deep caring for all of my clients because of our intimate connection through the healing work we do together. I am continually surprised and amazed at the miracles small and large that take place regularly in my work. There are so many gifts that we give each other through this way of being together.

"Everything is energy and that's all there is to it. Match the frequencies of the reality you want and you cannot help but get that reality. It can be no other way. This is not philosophy. This is physics."

—*Albert Einstein*

Chapter 12

Integrative Medicine:
A New Way of Healing

In the last 10 to 20 years, exceptionally high numbers of Americans have used alternative healing methods. Finally their voices are being heard around the country by doctors and hospitals as some have responded to their consumers' voices with new programs. We are beginning to realize that traditional Western (or allopathic) medicine and what is now being called integrative health care are often best when used together. I believe that our health care system will improve dramatically as we make this shift that includes a mind/body/spirit approach and that people will make great strides in their ability to heal as they pay attention to all aspects of their health.

Integrative Medicine Becoming Integrated

Integrative medicine can fill in the gaps by offering valid alternatives when Western medicine has no answers or treatment solutions for patients. Very often I've heard the story from people that a) the doctor doesn't know what is wrong with them, and b) they've just been sent home with nothing to help them (or maybe some pain meds that they don't want). It is extremely frustrating to be in this position, and it happens often. Then people go on the internet or try to find answers from some other source that may or may not be useful, or even safe. This is the perfect time to search for the integrative healing methods that are most appropriate for your situation. These methods can help encourage the body's own healing capacity in general which will assist the unknown problem from a macro perspective. Integrative methods can also assist by decreasing pain levels and fear, and by bringing comfort and support to the patient. A feeling of hopelessness is natural when one has an unknown illness, but it is not helpful for healing the body. Learning of other possibilities for healing and strengthening the body is beneficial emotionally as well as physically.

Especially in the last ten years, integrative medicine and specifically energy healing has become more widely known. I will speak about that modality here as it is the one I have the most experience with. As individuals and hospitals have begun using energy techniques, they are finding them to be powerful healing tools. I believe that energy healing will become commonplace over the next 10 to 15 years. It has been making its way into hospitals where the term integrative healthcare is used to describe a blend of what formerly were called Western (or allopathic) and alternative medicine.

The Twin Cities of Minneapolis and St. Paul in Minnesota are an example of a community using this kind of expanding health care. In 2012 there were at least 12 hospitals in the Twin Cities area that were offering some form of integrative healing services to their patients. These hospitals include Regions, St. John's, St. Joseph's, Woodwinds, Hennepin County Medical Center, Abbott-Northwestern, Children's Hospital and Clinics of Minneapolis, Fairview-Southdale, University of MN-Fairview, Mercy, Unity and St. Francis. Outside of the Twin Cities in Rochester, Minnesota, the well-known Mayo Clinic now has its own Integrative Healing Center.

Minneapolis is also lucky to have the Penny George Institute for Health and Healing. This is the largest hospital-based program of its kind in the country. They are setting national standards for enhancing health care through an integrative approach. They blend complementary therapies, integrative medicine and conventional Western medicine. They also provide services to both inpatients and outpatients. In addition, they educate healthcare professionals and teach community members about health promotion and self-healing practices. They also conduct research to identify best practices of integrative health and the impact of these services on health care costs.

In 2011 in St. Louis Park a new cancer facility opened called the Frauenshuh Cancer Center. Its mission and values are that of the Park Nicollet system, which encourages the head and heart working together. They offer a variety of classes and support groups for patients as well as support services such as individual and family counseling, music therapy with guided imagery, social work services and spiritual care. They also offer integrative therapies in the patient's rooms including healing touch, reflexology, acupuncture, reiki, massage therapy, yoga and qigong. These offerings are a blend of Eastern and Western therapies and the oncologists there have great respect for the effects of these therapies.

I can personally attest to the powers of energy healing before and after surgery, as I have been working on clients in that realm for more than 12 years. In many cases it was with people who had the treatment only after their surgery, but they still showed a significant difference in their healing time as compared to people who have not had any energy work. I've found that most people using energy healing seem to heal in half to two-thirds of the time it takes for those who don't experience the energy work. I am basing that on the surgeon's time-table for healing from a particular surgery, and on the patients' expectations for their own healing. Many patients and doctors have been surprised at how quickly some of my clients have healed, and by the reduced pain medication that was needed in their recovery. In general, for post-surgical patients the length of time a patient is in pain, and the intensity of that pain, is significantly reduced by energy work.

If hospitals would hire energy healers to work on those people who chose to have energy healing done before and certainly after their surgeries, it would be a win-win situation for both the patients and the hospitals. The patients would have the potential to heal more quickly and fully, with less pain involved, and the hospitals would then have another room to fill more quickly with other patients. It could promote better healing for the patients and a faster turnaround could mean more money for the hospitals. For this to happen there needs to be more education about what energy healing is and what the benefits are so that people understand the possibilities for their recovery. I am attempting to provide some of those answers here.

One of my teachers, Shelli Stanger-Nelson, was the principal investigator at Fairview-Southdale Hospital in Minneapolis in a study to learn the effects of energy healing on total joint replacements for knees or hips. Seventy-five subjects were randomly placed into control or treatment groups, divided fairly evenly between men and women. The protocol for the treatment group was to receive four energy healing sessions given by Stanger-Nelson. There was a statistically significant improvement in those who received the treatments, over those who did not receive the treatments in the areas of strength and endurance, range of motion, pain management and incisional healing.

I hope that in my lifetime allopathic medicine and energy healers will collaborate on a regular basis for the betterment of their patients, and for a more thorough and integrative approach to health and healing of the entire human being.

Research trials support the existence of electro-magnetic energy fields. The healing effects of energy work have been documented in a variety of research studies related to all different areas of healing. Rev. Rosalyn Bruyere was involved in several research projects that used hands-on-healing during the 1980s and 1990s. She studied the effects of energy healing on cardiac patients, AIDS patients, breast cancer patients, and cocaine babies, to name a few. Several if not all of these studies were in collaboration with medical doctors. The results were favorable for energy healing as a positive part of the healing process. Research done by others has included energy work with chronic pain, depression, diabetes, pain and joint mobility experienced by patients with total knee replacements, dementia, and electrodermal testing to measure the effects of healing touch treatments. This is just a sampling, not an exhaustive list of the research that has been done in this area.

Two of the leading energy healers and teachers in the United States are the Rev. Rosalyn Bruyere and Barbara Ann Brennan. It is interesting to note the background of both of these women before they became energy healers. Rev. Bruyere was trained as an electrical engineer (and energy in the body is in many ways like an electrical system) before becoming a healer, and Barbara Ann Brennan was a research scientist for NASA before becoming a psychotherapist and healer. I feel lucky to have trained with Rev. Bruyere, and she is certainly one of the smartest people I've ever met and has *amazingly* strong energy.

Energy and Healing

There is much to be said about energy as it pertains to the human body. I hope to give you enough understanding to make sense of what it means in regard to healing the body. For me, energy healing has been one of the great vehicles for working with myself and others to become more conscious about our health. The very nature of energy healing is a holistic approach that works with mind, body and spirit healing, and includes how they relate to each other. If you are interested in the information I give you here, there are innumerable books on the topic of energy healing that can give you much more. A complete list of related books as resources for this entire book will be provided at the end.

Energy healing is sometimes called Healing Touch, Therapeutic Touch, Hands-on-Healing, Bio-Energy Healing or Spiritual Healing, all meaning something very similar, with a few technical differences. Basically they refer to the practice of using a healer's hands and the healer's connection to his or her energy source (for example Earth, God or the Divine) to work with a client who wishes to receive healing energy beyond their own resources. The purpose is to bring the client into a place of balance, strength and wholeness within their mind, body and spirit by using techniques that may require healing hands on or off the body. A person lies on a massage table, fully clothed to receive this work, and it usually lasts somewhere between an hour or ninety minutes. The work is uniquely different each session and is something that cannot really be explained; it must be experienced, although it can be described simply as relaxing and pleasant.

The reasons to do energy healing are as varied as there are health issues. From a physical point of view, people can use the gift of energy healing for any health problem, from a cut on their finger or bump on their head, to headaches or fatigue. It can be used on people with arthritis, colitis, Alzheimer's, hypertension and heart disease, broken bones, viruses and infections, organ problems, pain and even cancer. It can also be used to clear physical trauma from an injury such as a sprained ankle or a knee, neck or back injury. Every form of disease could benefit from energy healing because it is a way to bring an imbalance in the body back to a state of balance, and to give the body more energy to work with, which increases circulation and encourages the body to focus on the problem area. This usually has the effect of speeding up the healing process.

Emotionally and spiritually, energy work can be used to help people clear trauma from their body memory. What this means is that when a person experiences physical abuse, sexual abuse, an accident of some kind, or some other trauma, there is good evidence that the memory of this experience is also stored somewhere in the body. It used to be thought that we just stored memories in the brain, but many studies now indicate that in addition to the brain we store these memories of our experiences and traumas in our body tissues, and sometimes in the chakras (energy centers) themselves. (I will give an explanation about the chakras later in this chapter.)

I have worked with a survivor of rape named Patricia Weaver Francisco who explains in her moving memoir called *Telling: A Memoir of Rape and Recovery*, how the energy healing we did helped her body memory of the incident become integrated into her whole being. Patricia Weaver Francisco writes that although she had done ten years of therapy prior to meeting me, she was unable to completely heal and integrate this event in her life until she went deeper into her body, where the emotional charge had been festering. In the process of doing energy work, the whole being is addressed in the healing, so the trauma can be healed on all levels, including the mental (or psychological), emotional, spiritual *and* body levels.

During this work difficult emotions such as anger, grief, anxiety and depression can come out of the unconscious mind of the client and into a conscious place where the client is assisted through their process of integrating and healing by an energy healer. Sometimes this involves a lot of talking at the same time that energy work is being done, and other times it is very quiet and very relaxing. As a healer, being there to witness, validate and have compassion for someone's experience is extremely important to the healing of that client's pain. During an energy session, a client may experience a surprising emotional release, sometimes one they don't associate with a story or memory, one that is just a release occurring without connection to the brain. This can be a very cathartic experience. Energy healing can also help a person to learn to feel deep relaxation and typically leaves a person with a feeling of being balanced and centered again – a feeling of calm and of well-being. Often my clients say that they feel "lighter", as if some weight has been lifted from them.

Healers are also using energy work with mental and spiritual issues such as depression, obsessive compulsive behaviors, or lack of connection with a higher power or some sort of faith. The body is not separate from these things. In fact, each layer of the energy field gives us information about what is going on with a person physically, emotionally, mentally and spiritually, and they all affect each other. Most often we are working with someone holistically on an issue involving all of these parts. When a shift occurs in the emotional body, it can often be accompanied by a shift in the physical body. When a person wishes to heal on all levels, energy work is effective, especially when done regularly. For instance, it may be received once a week or every other week for a period of time, or once a month while a person is working on a particular difficult pattern; or energy healing can be used for crisis situations, surgeries or unmanageable health problems whenever they come up. The regularity of the sessions can bring about a palpable change in people, affecting their whole lives, and often gives them a different frame of reference, typically the "big picture view". They can become more flexible and creative in finding solutions to things that have been keeping them stuck in certain areas of their lives. Many people who experience energy healing develop more love and acceptance of self, an ability to maintain deeper connections with others, and real gratitude for their existence.

Energy Healing and the Energy Body

Over the last 5,000 years there have been traditions from all over the world that have observed and studied energy fields with each culture calling it something different and finding its own interpretation. People living in ancient China and India knew about life force, *chi* or energy. In his book *Future Science,* Dr. John White lists 97 cultures that refer to the auric phenomena with 97 different names. Our energy field (or auric or biofield) is electromagnetic in nature and is created by the simultaneous movement of energy up and down the central channel of the body and in and out the seven chakras. There are texts that explain this phenomenon for those who wish to explore it more deeply, but for our purpose here I will give a somewhat less scientific version of the nature of energy fields and the energy body.

To begin, let us start with the idea that there is something called the Universal Energy Field as explained by Barbara Ann Brennan in her book *Hands of Light*. In this book she states that Dr. John White and Dr. Stanley Krippner list many properties of the Universal Energy Field. They say that it "permeates all space, animate and inanimate objects, and connects all objects to each other; it flows from one object to another; and its density varies inversely with the distance from its source. It also follows the laws of harmonic inductance and sympathetic resonance. Visual observations reveal the field to be highly organized in a series of geometric points, isolated pulsating points of light, spirals, webs of lines, sparks and clouds. It pulsates and can be sensed by touch, taste, smell and with sound and luminosity perceivable to the higher senses."

Next, let us look at the Human Energy Field (HEF), which is the part of the Universal Energy Field that is associated with the human body. This field, which is often called the "aura" or biofield, consists of seven layers that come off of the human body, interpenetrating each other in successive layers. Each layer has its own particular function and looks different from the others. The HEF is always associated with some form of consciousness, ranging from highly developed to very primitive. Drs. White and Krippner go on to say that the "The Human Energy Field has an organizing effect on matter and builds forms. It appears to exist in more than three dimensions. Any changes in the material world are preceded by a change in this field." This last sentence is important. What it means is that before a physical change occurs in the body, there is an indication of this change in the energy field around the person's body.

Some healers are able to see this field, while others feel these different layers as they are doing energy work. In Barbara Ann Brennan's book, *Hands of Light,* she shows each layer as it has been perceived by her after years of working with energy fields. She is a healer with higher sense perception, which many of us have. Many people have clairvoyance, which is being able to see things that others cannot see, or clairaudience, which is hearing things other people cannot hear, or clairsentience, which is being able to feel things that other people cannot feel.

The following are the seven layers or dimensions of the Human Energy Field that most healers agree on at this time in the evolution of this knowledge base (in the United States).

1) The first layer, the etheric layer, is most closely associated with the physical body. It is related to physical sensation such as pain or pleasure.

2) The next layer is related to the emotional body and it is associated with feelings.

3) The third layer relates to the mental body and is associated with thoughts and mental processes.

4) The fourth layer is the astral body, which is associated with the heart chakra. It also acts as a bridge for all energy to pass through when going from one world (body) to another (spirit). It is a place of transformation.

5) The fifth, sixth and seventh layers are associated with the spiritual dimensions of the person, each with a little different consciousness.

As you move from the layer closest to the body to each subsequent layer moving farther out from the body, each one becomes a finer energy, with higher vibrations than the layer that it surrounds and interpenetrates. And each one of these layers or dimensions are associated with a chakra (an energy center *within* the body).

Exercise to Feel Energy

Before we go any further I would like to give you a brief opportunity to feel your own energy field. This is a quick, fun exercise that I do with people in my classes, so that they can feel their own or someone else's energy field.

- First sit in a chair with your feet flat on the floor. Take three (or more) deep breaths, releasing any stress or tension you may feel as you exhale. Take your time.
- Then rub your hands together for about 30 seconds.
- Then spread your hands apart about 5-7 inches, moving them in and out a bit. You're trying to feel a magnetism, or resistance, or possibly buzzing or tingling in your hands. Can you feel anything like that? Now move your hands apart even farther, maybe three feet or so. Bring them in slowly until you feel like you've just hit a "wall" of energy or a magnetic resistance. This is your aura, or energy field.

We all have an energy field around our body. Our energy field or auric field is part of us and is connected to us. Some people are more sensitive to this phenomenon than others, but it is interesting to notice how our physical awareness goes beyond our physical body to include the subtle energies of the body.

Now we will look at another part of the energy body that is *inside* the body, called the chakras. (In addition, there is a third part of the energy body called the meridian system, which is the system used by Traditional Chinese Medicine to rebalance, strengthen and heal organs through acupuncture or other means. That is a different and complicated system that we will not explore here.)

Chakras

So what is a chakra? Anodea Judith, PhD, an authority on chakras who wrote *Wheels of Life*, defines the word chakra as "coming from the Sanskrit word for 'wheel' or 'disc' (some call a chakra a 'vortex'). Chakras spin in a wheel-like manner, sending energy out from the core of the body, and they assimilate energy from outside (the body) that enters the core. A chakra is an organizational center for the reception, assimilation, and the transmission of life energy."

Just as there are seven layers that make up our energy field, there are also seven main chakras or energy centers *within* the body. There are also secondary chakras and minor chakras, but for our purposes here, we will just talk about the seven main chakras because the whole concept of chakras is complex, and this is meant to be an introduction. Chakras are not seen as a physical characteristic, though people with the gift of clairvoyance can see them, and those with the gift of clairsentience can feel their presence. Chakras are instead subtle energies that now can be validated as the evolution of subtle-energy technologies has emerged so we can measure their existence and functions.

For the scientist, these spinning chakras are electromagnetic wave generators, each creating a particular frequency that can be measured in Hertz. These frequencies or wave forms can be seen as colors by an auric reader (clairvoyant). Each chakra corresponds with the color that the Hertz frequency creates. In 1988 at UCLA, Dr. Valerie Hunt and Rev. Rosalyn Bruyere carried out a study that was the first of its kind to validate the existence of the seven chakras that clairvoyant people have seen and described throughout the centuries. As Rev. Bruyere notes in her book *Wheels of Light – A Study of the Chakras* "Their research presented empirical data regarding the frequencies and actual functionings of all the chakras."

The study was called "A Study of Structural Neuromuscular Energy Field and Emotional Approaches" and was meant to study the effects of rolfing on the body and psyche. Rolfing is a form of bodywork that uses deep manipulation of the body's soft tissue to realign and balance the body's myofascial structure. Dr. Hunt utilized EMG electrodes (ordinarily used to measure the electrical potential of muscles) to study bioelectrical energy variations in areas of skin corresponding to the positions of the chakras. Barbara Ann Brennan writes about the following research in her book *Hands of Light*.

> She (Dr. Hunt) recorded the frequency of low millivoltage signals from the body during a series of rolfing sessions. To make these recordings she used elementary electrodes made of silver/silver chloride placed on the skin. Simultaneously with the recording of the electronic signals, Rev. Rosalyn Bruyere observed the auras of both the rolfer and the person being rolfed. Her comments were recorded on the same tape recorder as the electronic data. She gave a running report of the color, size and energy movements of the chakras and auric clouds involved.
>
> The scientists then mathematically analyzed the wave patterns recorded by a Fourier analysis and a sonogram frequency analysis. Both revealed remarkable results.
>
> Consistent wave forms and frequencies correlated specifically with the colors Rev. Bruyere reported. In other words, when Rev. Bruyere observed blue in the aura at any specific location, the electronic measurements would always show the characteristic blue wave form and frequency in the same locations. Dr. Hunt repeated the same experiment with seven other aura readers. They also saw auric colors that correlated with the same frequency/wave patterns.
>
> The following chart shows the color/frequency correlations as measured in Hertz or Hz = cycles/second:

Blue	*250-275 Hz plus 1200 Hz*
Green	*250-475 Hz*
Yellow	*500-700 Hz*
Orange	*950-1050 Hz*
Red	*1000-1200 Hz*
Violet	*1000-2000 Hz plus 300-400; 600-800*
White	*1100-2000 Hz*

These frequency bands, except for the extra bands at blue and violet, are in reverse order of rainbow color frequency. The frequencies measured are a signature of the instrumentation as well as the energy being measured.

Dr. Hunt says, "Throughout the centuries in which sensitives have seen and described the auric emissions, this is the first objective electronic evidence of frequency, amplitude and time, which validates their subjective observation of color discharge." (*Hands of Light* by Barbara Ann Brennan, pgs. 33-34.)

To get a better understanding of the chakras, the following is a simplified chart showing some of the main aspects of consciousness associated with each chakra, as well as the color and element associated with each. Anatomically, each major chakra is associated with a major nerve plexus and glandular center within the endocrine system of the body. Each is also associated with a particular physiologic system. There are several other correspondences such as body parts and organs associated with each chakra, foods, sounds, etc., but because my purpose is to give you a general understanding, I will only include some basic information.

Chakra One: Color is red. Located at the base of the spine. It is the generator of life force energy, and is associated with the physical body, survival, and your grounding connection to the earth. Its element is earth.

Chakra Two: Color is orange. Located just below the belly button. It is associated with emotions, flow and change, sexuality and clairsentience. Its element is water.

Chakra Three: Color is yellow. Located in the solar plexus. It is associated with our self-esteem, power, will and how we mentally process the world around us. Its element is fire.

Chakra Four: Color is green.   Located in the heart area. It is associated with love, relationship, breath, and balance. It is also the place of transformation and integration between the lower three physical chakras and the upper three spiritual chakras. Its element is air.

Chakra Five: Color is blue.   Located in the throat. It is associated with communication, sound, creativity and knowing when to act or speak. Its element is sound.

Chakra Six: Color is violet/purple.   Located in the center of the forehead. It is associated   with intuition, insight, imagination and seeing (or clairvoyance). Its element is light.

Chakra Seven: Color is white. Located at the top of the head. This is the place where we connect with God or our Higher Self, and link with it to become something greater than ourselves. It is associated with knowledge, thought, understanding, and transcendence (meditation.)   Its element is thought.

Each of the layers of the energy field is associated with one of the chakras and connects with it numerically. For example, the first layer of the field has a similar descriptive consciousness to the first chakra. They both relate to the physical body and have to do with life force energy.   In looking at the chart above and then at the layers of the energy field on page 170, you will see the relationship between the two. The system as a whole creates an electromagnetic field (or auric field) that includes the seven layers and the seven chakras.

Basically chakras bring in universal life force energy, spiritual and psychic energy and assimilate it, disperse it throughout the body and then transform it into physical energy. We also use our chakras to send energy *out* from our core. These energy centers or chakras vitalize all parts of our being. Physiologically the chakras appear to be involved with the flow of higher energies through specific energetic channels into the cellular structure of the physical body. This energy in turn, translates into glandular-hormonal output, which subsequently affects the entire physical body. The chakras also help to regulate the flow of vital energy into different organs of the body. With proper functioning, chakras help to establish strength and balance in a particular physiologic system. Conversely, abnormal chakra function can create weakness in an area of the body or in a particular organ. (This does not mean that abnormalities within the chakra system are the only cause of illness. There are other influences such as chemical, bacterial, viral and environmental factors that can also create disease in the physical body.)

Anatomically, each major chakra is associated with a major nerve plexus and endocrine gland along with a physiological system. The following diagram will show a summary of these relationships. It starts with the first chakra and works its way up to the seventh.

Chakra	Nerve Plexus	Physiological System	Endocrine System
Coccygeal	Sacral-Coccygeal	Reproductive	Gonads
Sacral	Sacral	Genitourinary	Leydig
Solar Plexus	Solar	Digestive	Adrenals
Heart	Heart Plexus	Circulatory	Thymus
Throat	Cervical Ganglia Medulla	Respiratory	Thyroid
Third Eye	Hypothalamus Pituitary	Autonomic Nervous System	Pituitary
Head	Cerebral Cortex Pineal	CNS Central Control	Pineal

Source: *Vibrational Medicine* by Richard Gerber, MD, pg. 130.

Chakras also transmit energy between one another through passageways in the tips of the chakras, which are connected energetically inside the body near the spine. Chakras are not physical, but instead are energetic in nature. Chakras can be thought of as gateways between various dimensions, meaning mind, body and spirit. The activity in each chakra affects, connects with and plays on the activity in the other.

When an event happens, for example when someone ends a relationship with you, your entire being responds, and this includes your chakras. Your third chakra, feeling a threat to your self-esteem, will constrict and send a message down to the first chakra to close because it does not feel safe "out there." Your heart chakra will contract as well, and in your body you may feel both your belly and your heart actually hurting. Your head may feel scrambled as you struggle to comprehend the situation because the seventh chakra, responsible for your thoughts, is not getting enough energy moving through it to help you process the situation. This is an illustration of how our chakras are working as a part of us all the time. The information that passes between them constantly affects our behavior and contributes to the creation of our personality.

Part of the role of the chakras is to bring about the development of different aspects of self-consciousness in each person. Each chakra relates to specific psychological functions and symbology that help us work with the issues that each person has of mind, body and spirit. The first three chakras have to do with our physical body, the fourth or heart chakra is the transformation point or bridge between those lower three chakras and the upper three chakras that have to do with our spiritual life. Chakras can be open or closed, excessive or deficient at any given time. Even though our chakras are always changing, it is important for us to open the chakras regularly and increase the flow of energy through them because the more energy that flows through them, the healthier we become. This can be done consciously or unconsciously. We can become ill when there is an imbalance of energy or blocked flow in the chakras for long periods of time.

To open your own chakras means you are helping them receive

energy from the outside world. There are a number of things you can do to open them, but only a couple that are simple enough to pass along in the context of this book. The first would be through meditation, where you would focus on each chakra separately starting with the first, possibly thinking of the color associated with that chakra (if this helps you), while spinning the chakra clockwise in your mind (you are the clock). (When a woman is menstruating her chakras spin counter-clockwise, otherwise chakras are supposed to be spinning clockwise.) You could also put your own hand in front of each chakra, spinning it clockwise, either in the context of a meditation or just doing that separately. This connects the secondary chakra in the hand with the main chakra, where it is encouraged to synchronize with the hand movement. Other ways our chakras tend to open is from meditating (even without consciously spinning them in a physical way), receiving a good massage, doing some sort of movement or exercise, sneezing or having an orgasm. The chakras that tend to be closed more often may not open completely from exercising, but it is still worth doing. All movement helps the body to move within, freeing up blockages and strengthening all of our physiological processes.

You would have the most success in opening your chakras if you worked with an energy healer. Learning what it feels like once a chakra has opened usually requires some practice and assistance. It is only after learning more about chakras that you would begin to know when one or more of your chakras are working optimally, or how you can determine that. There are more complex exercises which relate to opening each chakra that can be found in either Anodea Judith's book *Wheels of Life* or Barbara Ann Brennan's book *Hands of Light*.

Learning about the chakras can be complicated if you choose to really dig into it because it is an exercise in exploring your relationship to the many aspects of consciousness or psychological functions for each chakra and becoming aware of how they play out in your life. This is a deep study into your psyche and behavior; it is not light reading, but is very useful. I have taught a nine-month class on the seven chakras, and we could have easily gone longer considering the content we covered and the depth of the students' personal learning. Of course you don't have to go that deep into the learning to find the information extremely interesting. The following will give you a little introduction into the relationship between the chakras and your health.

Chakras and Our Health

So how do these chakras affect our health and why do energy healers work with them? We work with the energy field and the chakras because they give us information about what kind of balance or imbalance is present in the body (this would include mental and emotional bodies in addition to physical ones). A disease does not become a disease overnight. It takes varying amounts of time for problems in the body to actually manifest as physical symptoms. So if you are having a slight pain in your stomach area, for instance, and it continues for a week or two, you could choose to go to an energy healer who would assist the body in releasing an energy blockage and strengthen the energy in the third chakra (the stomach area) and probably in the whole body, thereby helping your stomach heal itself. It's possible that if you did not get any energy healing that that pain could continue and the problem would worsen until you go to a doctor and find out you have an ulcer. Had you stopped the process before it got to that point, it would have many advantages like saving yourself from pain, money and time expenditures. It is also possible that the pain would resolve itself on its own as well, but for something that has been bothering you for some time, energy healing is useful.

Sometimes the imbalance is not as clear as in the last example, and you might report that there seems to be something "off" in your body, but you're not sure what it is. An energy healer would scan the body to get information from it. An energy healer can tell if something is blocked up or has too much energy in it by doing a body scan, but that does not necessarily tell them what is wrong, just that there is an imbalance of some sort. That may be all a healer needs to know at that point, and if they can fix the imbalance by working with the energy field and chakras, a problem may be averted. As I mentioned earlier, the body flows like a river, it is a complex, amazing masterpiece of constant processes that happen without us knowing about them. If an imbalance should occur, it is likely that it will right itself given the proper environment. Sometimes all it takes to create the proper environment is sleep, rest and good nutrition. Other times, help may be needed from an outside source like energy healing, acupuncture, or a certain supplement or homeopathic remedy to give the body a little push toward healing and homeostasis.

Each of our chakras affects the surrounding physical body, so when an area or organ in the body becomes problematic it is very likely that the chakra in that area is off balance and not properly functioning. Again, by the time an organ is not working well, the dysfunction of the chakra and also the physical body has been present for some time. The state of imbalance of the chakras can cause physical symptoms or disease, no matter if it's a headache or heart disease.

Before a physical problem occurs in the body, the body's energy field is the first to become out of balance. Then the chakra in that particular area (or possibly more than one) will go out of balance. If these two parts of the energy body do not correct themselves, the problem can then go into the physical body. The physical body, being more dense than the energy body, takes a longer time to manifest a noticeable problem. When the problem or imbalance is in one of the energy bodies (the energy field or a chakra), it is much easier to correct, since it is easier to balance and change energy patterns than it is to change matter (meaning physical tissue). By the time the pattern of imbalance reaches the physical tissue, is has become more established because it has been present everywhere (in the energy field, chakras and physical body) for a longer period of time. Unfortunately, this means that it will take more time to reverse the imbalance.

So when a body is trying to restore tissue or a broken bone for example, the energy field (aura) of that bone is disrupted as well as the surrounding chakras (most likely secondary or even minor ones). Having energy work done in that area, on both the energy field and the associated chakras, strengthens the "intelligence" of the bone, reminding it of its boundaries, structure and the matrix that forms the bone, while also encouraging healing by increasing the circulation to the area.

Another function of the chakras is to bring about the development of the different aspects of consciousness that each is related to. Each chakra is associated with several aspects of consciousness or psychological functions. For example, the first chakra is concerned with survival and life force. If you came to me as a client and you were having anxiety and not feeling safe, I would know that these two states are related to the first chakra. I would then be able to ask you questions like "When did this start for you?", and "Was there a stressful event that happened to you at that time?" We may find that there was very good reason at the time for you to feel unsafe and to have anxiety, but now the situation has changed and yet the feelings still remain. This is the process of finding something that has been in your unconscious mind and bringing it up into consciousness, which is where it must be to work on and heal or integrate the issue. If you are not aware of what causes the feelings you're having, then you certainly cannot change them. Often there is a physical problem in the area where an energy blockage has remained for a long period of time, so energy work is important to strengthen and rebalance the chakra itself. We would also work together to create an updated belief, one that could bring more life force to the client. This would help reduce the symptoms of anxiety and fear by replacing them with a different internal voice.

For a physical issue such as a sore throat, one might assume a physical cause such as a virus, and that may well be. But sometimes a sore throat can come from a blockage in the fifth chakra, because the person with the sore throat has not been speaking up for themselves in a situation that has really been bothering them. After a period of time of being angry or upset and not saying so, he or she may manifest a sore throat. By not speaking up, the area could become compromised, which may make them vulnerable to contracting a virus. Or a person with a sore throat may find that it goes away "miraculously" when they address the issue by communicating their feelings or concerns, or as we healers say "speaking their truth."

The aspects of consciousness that pertain to each chakra are formed through our experiences, our perceptions, our behavior and our environment. Our chakras significantly affect the make-up of our personality. Everything we do or say creates our chakra's health or lack of it and affects the world around us. If we choose to change some of our old and unhealthy beliefs, we can also change the health of our chakras, and hence our personality may also shift. Anodea Judith says that:

What we generate (in our chakras) determines much of what we receive, and because of this it behooves us to work on our chakras and clean up outdated, dysfunctional or negative programming that may be getting in our way. By working with an energy healer to become more conscious of the beliefs that we hold, we can learn how to choose new thoughts, beliefs and behaviors that can actually change our physical, mental, emotional and spiritual health for the better. As we do this work, we may experience the opening of a chakra, and also realize a deeper understanding of what our own current state of consciousness is in that chakra. Being more conscious helps us to be more authentic.

Questions pertaining to your energy and chakra systems

1) Are you beginning to see how the whole system of the energy bodies and the physical body is really all one?

2) Can you imagine working on your maladies by using this system to create more health in your life?

3) What is a minor issue for you right now - physical, mental, emotional or spiritual - that by using the above information regarding the chakra system could help you become conscious of something that so far has been unconscious to you?

4) Are you aware of a particular area in your body that has been a "vulnerable" place for you for a long time? If yes why do you think that is?

5) Has your belief about problems in your body been that they are "random" events, or have you ever thought of the possibility that they may be connected to something currently going on in your life?

6) After looking at the chart of the chakras, can you see what chakras might be weaker or stronger in you?

7) Do the areas where you have had physical problems line up with what you may think of as your weaker chakras?

Body Symbology and its Clues for Healing

Body symbology is a tool for healing the body/mind connection. Using body symbology can be an access point for healing. It provides a way for us to listen to the messages of our body to find a deeper understanding. Healers who have been working with people on their mind/body/spirit relationships and the healing of them for many years have given us these symbols that we can check with to become more aware of the possible meanings of problems we are having within our physical body.

A symbol can be a material (meaning "matter" or physical) representation of immaterial qualities or functions. A symbol can also awaken us to a perception in our world (and in particular in our body/mind) that may make us aware of some specific knowledge contained in our soul. Some say our body is the soul presented in its richest and most expressive form. The key to symbology is to look at what that body part does and notice how that symbolism may be playing out in our mind/body/spirit in terms of a difficulty with it. For example, our legs move us forward in life so when there is a problem with our legs it could mean that we are having some fear about moving forward in a particular aspect of our life.

Body symbology is not a science or absolute truth. But it is worth paying attention to as a guide or directional tool. The soul cares about connection, relatedness, and exploring. It is the mind that wants facts, as does modern science. But medicine's analytical nature is breaking down the connectedness between our mind, body and spirit, and I believe this is a major impediment to our ability to heal. Body symbology is really about listening to the messages of the body to find a deeper understanding. The symptom or the disease in us can be the cure, because it can reconnect us with who we are once we have strayed from our essence.

Chakras and physical symptoms are often tied together because of their placement in the body and the purpose or meaning of that area or body part. This was alluded to in the earlier discussion on the connection of body symptoms with chakras. The example about the source of the sore throat used this way of thinking for exploring the existence of the sore throat. As another example, the intestines are used for taking in food, assimilating and absorbing the proper nutrients and releasing the rest as waste. The second and third chakras are in the area of the intestines, and they also have a similar job, though not only in the literal sense of processing food. They also deal with our ability to assimilate and absorb experiences, emotions and thoughts that are healthy for us and to release or let go of those that are not. If someone is suffering from constipation or colitis, they may be having an internal issue around their ability to absorb or release experiences in a healthy way. It could be just a short-term problem or it could become a habit or ingrained pattern. That would depend first on whether that person is consciously wanting to change the problem, and secondly on their ability to shift internally or externally through a behavior or action and come back to balance in their digestion (of life).

When clients have a specific body complaint, I may ask them if they're interested in looking at the body symbology as a way of getting more information around the issue. I will tell them what the symbology is for a certain body part or organ and then ask questions to see if we can make a connection between what is going on in their life and what is bothering them physically. Once someone sees a relationship between the two, they have become conscious about a connection they hadn't seen before, and sometimes that is all they need to make a shift. It can be one of those "aha" moments where realizing what is going on makes perfect sense and then the person can let go of the physical symptom because they understand why they're having it, and they can validate themselves and give themselves compassion for responding in that way. Other times we need to do some processing about that connection and about the issue, which can be much easier to change while I work on the chakra that it connects with at the same time we process mentally. Often the person will assist the process of shifting internally by using an affirmation both out loud during the work we are doing, and by saying and/or writing it at home. This can be very powerful work.

For example, let's say someone comes to see me and has a very sore right foot that was not injured; it has just been hurting for a couple of weeks. I would tell them that our feet are about our foundations, our roots, and they are our base that supports us and move us. Sometimes our feet are about family issues and parents in particular, or anything that is foundational to our lives. Then I would ask questions about these areas to see if any of them relate to that person's life at the moment. Someone may respond that they lost their job recently or that their father has been very sick. These responses would make sense as an unconscious reason for their right foot to be feeling out of sorts.

There are two other parts of symbology that can help people to discern why they are experiencing a certain symptom or what it might be about. The lower part of the body (below the waist) can correspond to the past, and the upper part can correspond to the future (above the waist). (Remember these are just hints to aid in our search for meaning). What I find more useful though, is that the right and left sides of the body have to do with masculine and feminine aspects of life. For instance, the right side is related to masculine aspects; either a male in your life or the masculine parts of yourself like your work, or the "doing" part of your life. The right side also pertains to your physical body.

The left side of the body has to do with feminine aspects; either a female in your life, or a feminine part of yourself like mothering, relationships, or the "idea" part of yourself, as well as the emotional body/self. When you are able to put together the masculine/feminine aspects with a body part's purpose, sometimes you will see that an injury to a certain area makes all the sense in the world. For example, say you sprained your left ankle while on a trip with your sister who you were having relationship trouble with. It may or may not have been an accident that you twisted that ankle while with her. It may have happened to bring conscious attention to the problem within your relationship, and come up symbolically to represent that issue. Or that your right knee hurt after losing a big contract at work, knees being about ego and competition. I have come to believe in this idea of symbology because I have seen it make sense with me and with others over and over again.

After my car accident I had an x-ray taken of my whole spine and related areas. The x-ray showed that I had developed a fairly large cyst in my clavicle. I was then sent to an orthopedic surgeon who told me he thought it was made of bone and that it had been there a while, "probably since you were 10" (which was how old I was when my parents got divorced). He said he could cut a part of my hip out and then replace this piece of my clavicle with the hip bone. I reminded him that this cyst didn't cause me any pain and said that we would not be doing that surgery. He resigned himself but told me to come back in six months so that he could check if it had grown.

During that time I went home and read *You Can Heal Your Life* by Louise L. Hay. This book talks about how you can heal and change aspects of your life that are holding you back and keeping you from being the person you want to be by using affirmations. There is also a section on body symbology that lists physical problems and body parts like acne, addictions, sciatica, legs, the eyes, the back, different organs, etc. In the next column it states the probable cause (metaphysically) for a person having an issue in that area or of that kind, and in the last column it gives you an affirmation to work with to heal the problem.

I tell you all of this because I looked up what the book said about cysts and tumors, words that were both used by the doctor to describe this thing in my clavicle. What the book says regarding the likely reason for cysts and tumors was dead on, as was the timing of when he said this "cyst" probably started growing. I will share with you the explanations for these two conditions, and the affirmations that went with them. See if you notice the correspondence. "Tumors..... Nursing old hurts and shocks, building remorse. Affirmation: I lovingly release the past and turn my attention to this new day. All is well." The explanation for cysts was "Running the old, painful movie. Nursing hurts. A false growth." And the affirmation: "The movies of my mind are beautiful because I choose to make them so. I love me." I thought it was amazing how perfectly these words fit with my having this extra boney thing in my body. I said these affirmations every day, and I wrote them often, over and over again. Six months later I went back to see the surgeon, and he took another x-ray. It turned out that the cyst had shrunk to half its original size. He was flabbergasted! He said he had no idea how that thing could have gotten smaller and that he'd never seen that happen before, but I figured I knew why.

I started using a lot of these affirmations on myself for the many aches and pains I had from my car accident, as well as the affirmations that were used to change the broader picture of one's life, and they seemed to make a real difference for me. It seems that for my clients and for me, about 90-95% of the time the explanations that Louise Hay gives in her book make perfect sense for a given situation. It is but one tool, and many people can find the wisdom in using it. For some, using affirmations doesn't work, and that is okay. We all have our own ways of dealing with emotional processes. (There is a shortened version of Louise Hay's book that is called *You Can Heal Your Body* that is just the list with metaphysical causes and affirmations but without the rest of the information on changing other parts of your life, e.g. relationships or career.)

Chapter 13

Jane's Healing Story

Before I go into Jane's story I want to lay out a little groundwork. All people are wounded in some way, and sometimes these wounds affect our health. We have come from imperfect families with imperfect parents because all of us are imperfect, including the person who is reading this right now. That is the nature of humanity. In my opinion our job is to break through the bonds of our wounding to find our true nature, our real gifts, our purpose on earth so that we can make this earth a better place for all. I tell this story to inspire you to look at this aspect in yourself and your life, and to show you how it's done well.

As you read this remember it is not in the details where the message lies, but in the story as a whole. You also have a story of wounding and hopefully a story of healing that may or may not have some similarities to Jane's story. But if you have not yet worked with this in your life there is still time. As Jane did, you may also wait until you are faced with a huge motivating reason to fix what is broken in you, or you could start now. There is no shame in realizing your weaknesses. We all have them. The downfall is in denying that there is anything hard or real to look at. It would be more wise to become conscious of those weaknesses and attempt to make them right so that you can be happier and feel more free in your life.

Jane

I met Jane as the coach of my son's soccer team and as the mother of one of my son's friends. We knew each other for four years before our healing work happened and became friends during that time. Our family spent New Year's Eve of 2011 together with her family. In February 2011 she told me that she had been diagnosed with breast cancer. She asked me if I would help her during her healing process and I said I would. I honestly never had the thought that her cancer would get the best of her, even at the first moment I heard about it. She is a strong, fit, tough woman, and I believed in her ability to heal. But she had to do the work, and I was honored to help her through it.

The part about this story that could be similar to many others is that sometimes the family systems we grow up in are so unhealthy that we manifest some kind of condition, addiction or disease. This is exactly what happened in Jane's case, and her story illustrates how strong the mind/body connection can be. She feels that the emotional toll that it took to grow up in her family of origin is the reason for her cancer. She believes that the cancer was her own manifestation of blocked emotions from that abusive family system. The following are her words, and the details of the psychological profiles and defense systems of her and her parents. It is in these personal accounts where the wisdom for healing can be found. Sometimes you have to dig deep, and Jane was not only aware of that, she showed up completely and did what it took to survive, and she continues to work with these patterns still.

Jane was the youngest of four children in her family. Her father was the architect of their family system, making all the rules for the family. He had been terribly abused as a child. Both of her parents were narcissists who were not clear about their own identity, so they would use their children to make themselves feel good. They did not allow their children to be separate entities from themselves. When the children tried, they would be punished, shamed or abused physically,

190

verbally, emotionally and sometimes sexually. For Jane, this set up a pattern of holding fear in her body. She was not allowed to speak up or to be herself. If she did, her parents would put her down or discount her, or physically hurt her or otherwise do whatever they needed to do to make themselves feel good and to fill their own emptiness. They couldn't provide their own internal happiness, so they got it externally from their kids.

Jane lived in fear of this abuse as a child, and it forced her to be constantly vigilant so she could notice if she was in danger. She learned to do exactly what her parents wanted her to do or to hide. She often coped with a situation by hiding if she felt she was in danger. As she became an adult, this coping mechanism was no longer useful. However, her body still held fear and she believes that holding in this fear is what created the blockage in her body that made the cancer.

When she was 17 she realized that she had to make sound decisions about the trajectory of her life, and yet she had no idea how to do that because she had a life suited to her parents' needs instead of her own. She felt she had no base or sense of self from which to make difficult decisions. She acted out with food by either over-eating or by being bulimic. She tried drinking and some drugs which didn't suit her, but the fear came back harder and she realized she had no self of her own, no emotional base. She tried going to college, but realized she was living in a shell that protected and hid her, and that she was lost. She was completely depressed, had bulimia and a spastic colon. Despite her dad's threats about leaving school, she dropped out and lived with her sister.

She then started working and put herself through therapy. As she would talk in therapy about growing up in her family, she would have big releases of fear that actually made her body feel like it was frozen in fear like a rabbit. She would be unable to talk and her teeth would chatter during the releases. She also had this fear response in work situations if she was unable to deal with them, and she'd go into her child self. During her 20s and 30s she was trying to learn to speak her own truth, have her own power in the world, and continued searching for what she needed. She realized in therapy that a huge family rule was that if you told the real story about the family you would be in BIG trouble. Her father was a well-known physician, so telling the truth about what was really going on in the family was completely forbidden because showing your problems was a weakness. All her life she held in that truth to protect herself from her dysfunctional parents. And she lived with the fear of being exactly who she needed to be.

She didn't realize how blocked she was and how much more fear she had to deal with until she was diagnosed with breast cancer. Then she felt a basic primal fear of dying, a fight or flight fear, in addition to her first wounding of fear in her childhood. She could feel it, taste it and experience the fear constantly, to the point that she couldn't sleep for a period of time, which was unusual for her. Jane continued with therapy before and after her diagnosis. She felt strongly that she had to work through this fear and now this anger. She was so angry that she got cancer despite how healthy she was living. She generally ate healthy food (other than some sugar and artificial sweetener), exercised almost every day, took vitamins, went to a chiropractor, laughed a lot and had wonderful children that made her happy. The cancer made her feel trapped again just like she felt at home in her childhood, plus she wasn't ready to die. Being an extremely physical, athletic person she felt that cancer was a good expression of dis-ease for her to conquer because she could handle a lot of physical stress and push herself physically. She used this strength to get over her initial fear, so she could move forward with the deep internal healing of her mental/mind and spirit realms.

With the cancer diagnosis Jane became aware that she had to pay attention to the emotional work that was necessary to move forward. The cancer was a motivating force for her to clear what was still not healed from her body/mind/spirit. It pushed her to lift the fog of denial and allowed her to see more clearly so she could get to the core of her fears learned in childhood.

She realized that she had still been following the lesson from childhood that "you sacrifice yourself so someone else gets the good stuff," and if you don't you will be punished and then become helpless. Having a cancer diagnosis pushed her to see that she could no longer live by those old rules and that she would certainly not thrive if she continued to follow them. She felt that she could not afford to be in denial and that she had to do whatever it took to figure out where she was still blocked and heal it. Jane believes that you have to move forward in life and continually attempt to become a better person. She believes we each have a purpose. She wants to be free of this work so her soul will be free to experience different things.

The Work of Healing

After Jane's surgery to remove the cancer cells in her breast tissue, she found out that there were also cells in some lymph nodes. This meant that she would have to have both chemotherapy and radiation. It was during the rest and strength-building period just following her surgery and before her chemotherapy started that we began with the energy work.

While I did energy healing on her body she spoke to me of her childhood, her defenses to maintain her sanity, her fears and pain. She had a very good psychological handle on the situation, not only from doing her own therapy but also from having a sister who is a psychotherapist with whom she processes these issues too. What we needed to get down to was the deeply held memories in her tissue and organs. She feels that the cancer brought to the surface the deep-seated trauma from her childhood and she knew she had to go there, even if it was really scary.

During the energy work we did she felt like she was dumping her cover (the things she had hidden to stay safe) and the debris and other old stuff that was covering up her core (essence). The cancer made her dig deeper to release this stuck garbage, and she felt the clearing that I did energetically scraped her clean. She experienced old memories of anger that she felt were pulled out as I worked on her energy body. She also experienced a lot of shame. As a child she was not allowed to have any needs. When she expressed a need her parents' response made her feel ashamed. Her shame shut her up as a kid, which actually kept her safe because if she had had anger she would be punished somehow. But this shame also kept her from being heard. Shame and neglect went together for her. Her core self was not allowed to grow because her parents always had to look good, but she couldn't look good. (She felt they took that from her for themselves.)

Jane had to basically raise herself, as her mother had been too weak to fight against her father's strong will. Her mother just did whatever she wanted to, staying up late and sleeping into the afternoon. In fact, she was unable to care for her four children, so they always had hired help to perform basic care-taking duties that her mother could not perform. During our process Jane was able to access the anger she had held inside from all of this. She realized the anger at her father who had set up this sick family system was a stepping stone for the anger she felt from the cancer. In other words, the rules she was forced to live by as a child were holding her down and making her sick, and she knew she couldn't let that happen anymore.

Because she has dug in so deep to process the emotional trauma, Jane is now finding more power. She continues to have breakthroughs as she clears emotional trauma and the process continues to get easier for her. She is learning what her true self is and to do what she's best at without being afraid. She still has some doubt and fear but it is different; it doesn't control her or immobilize her anymore.

Prior to Jane's chemo sessions I would go to her home for a half hour to prepare her for receiving the chemotherapy by:

1) Massaging her neck and shoulders

2) Running some energy into her to strengthen her body and energy field so she could better receive the chemo

3) Asking for help from her guides to help her open to and visualize the medicine going only to the cancer cells and leaving the healthy cells alone

4) Doing a blessing to keep her angels and guides with her as she received treatment

Jane felt that these sessions were really beneficial because they allowed her to let down her guard and work *with* the process of receiving chemotherapy and not against it. They enabled her to relax enough to allow that to happen. This also gave her a feeling of some sort of power within the process so that she was a participant instead of a victim who had to just let the treatments happen to her. (She was not happy to be receiving "poison" and we had to work with that term before she began the chemo so it could be seen in a more positive light.)

Once the chemotherapy began Jane received the energy healing on a more physical level, with no processing of emotions during our sessions like we had done prior to her chemo. This was because the chemo was so depleting it was all she could handle at the time. She did, however, continue with her psychotherapy during that time period and there was a lot of emotion that had come up to the surface to be healed. But immediately following the chemo, when she felt so physically raw and miserable, she just rested and took in the energy during our sessions. I would clear her body's energy field of the chemicals and reconnect her chakra system so her energy field could become strong and balanced again. She feels that because her energy system was "turned on" again regularly she was getting clearer messages about her feelings and a clearer vision as to how she needed to heal her past memories. She thinks that the combination of chemotherapy (which was a constant reminder of the fact that she had cancer and that trauma had blocked her system) and receiving energy healing pushed her to dig deeper into her feelings and ultimately made her mentally clearer. In psychotherapy she would think about and talk about her past. Once her energy body was clear, she felt she had another tool to work with that she hadn't gotten through psychotherapy. The energy work enabled Jane to integrate these events by becoming conscious on an emotional level of the effects of her past events in her family. The energy healing basically took her emotional awareness to another level of healing.

Jane still managed to work out about five days a week (instead of her usual six) during chemotherapy, which was really important to her. She would walk, slowly run, bike or swim, and always did some exercise in the morning before her chemo. After the chemo she would become fatigued, have "chemo brain" (i.e. foggy and unclear thinking), and was bothered by nausea for which she used meds, but she felt the energy work helped her to feel better more quickly after each chemo session. She believes that because her physical body was always strong, she came back quickly after our work together. She felt exhausted, but she never felt weak.

While she was receiving radiation, which happened five days a week for six and a half weeks (33 treatments), Jane worked out six days a week. She said it felt like nothing compared to the chemo and she even trained for and participated in a triathalon which included swimming, biking and running. I worked on her every other week during this time. I also sent her to another healer who worked with her several times and reported the radiation had seriously affected her immune system. Outwardly she got a nasty wound on her skin where the radiation had burned her, which apparently happens often during radiation treatment.

Jane's spiritual life has changed through this experience as well. She generally feels lighter and more connected to her core essence. She sees things more clearly and does not doubt herself like she used to. She feels like she is being led more by her intuition and stays with her true self more easily. She now has more awareness of her feelings of shame or fear so that she can recognize them quickly, label them as such, and allow the remaining feelings to move through her body instead of remaining stuck and causing a blockage. She has also begun a regular daily practice of meditation that lasts from five to fifteen minutes. She finds these meditations to be quite powerful as they keep her in regular contact with her divine essence.

Another benefit has been a stronger connection with both her spirit teacher and a Native American spirit guide that have always been with her. She now has the ability to feel their presence and they are always with her or near her. When she jumped in the water for her triathlon she said the Indian let out a war cry. She loved that!

Jane feels that the work we did together was invaluable. She is grateful for the teaching I gave her about the chakras and their purposes and it has helped deepen her learning and personal insights. Both Jane and I think that she looks younger, clearer, and we can feel and see the light within her. As of this writing (on her two-year anniversary of the diagnosis), Jane has received a clean bill of health from her doctors.

Jane's father died five months before she received her own diagnosis of cancer. His dying process proved to be a healing experience for her as she held great awareness of her ability to be completely loving with him. As she cared for him on his death bed he said to her that he had been a monster, and both she and her sister said yes, you were. But it was important to Jane that she have compassion and hold a loving space for him so he could leave feeling he was cared for and loved. This was a way for her to honor her own integrity and be true to herself.

"Happiness is not a matter of intensity but of balance and order and rhythm and harmony."

— *Thomas Merton*

Chapter 14

Balance

To be in balance in the different areas of our lives means to be in a state of equilibrium, and it is a much sought-after state in our American culture. We seem to be getting less and less discretionary time as daily living becomes more complex. Because of this we can begin to lose contact with important aspects of our lives through lack of time, which often leads us into a state of disconnection with our inner self. Oftentimes this can lead to imbalance in the direction of too much time spent on one area of life, for instance a career, or it can help us decide that we would rather live more simply. But in any case, creating the time for a well-balanced life has certainly become a challenge.

Sometimes there is not much of a choice in finding this equilibrium, for instance, when couples are starting their families or in the case of a single parent who may not have enough time to realistically live a balanced life. In situations like these it would be good to at least acknowledge that the intention is to move toward balance. With this realization it may become easier to bring about options that support a more balanced life. For example, a single mother could accept an offer from a friend who is willing to take her children for a weekend, thus giving her the time to rest or get things done that have been waiting to be completed.

As a new parent I recall a whole host of activities that didn't happen in my life for a period of time when my son was a baby and toddler. Caring for young children is one of those completely time-consuming jobs, and yet a time of sweetness and joy as well. I remember feeling like I was barely out in the world until my son was about three, but I knew it was a conscious choice that I made and that my life would again change back so that I felt more a part of the outside world. It was wonderful to get back to exercising regularly (out of the house), socializing more and working again.

Finding balance in daily living is a dynamic and fluid process. We are always moving either away or toward balance with each of our choices. If we can maintain some balance for a period of time that is a success. But equally important is to be aware of feeling or knowing that we're out of balance so that we can determine what it is that will help us come back to more equilibrium.

One of our challenges with noticing balance or lack of it comes from the fast pace of the lives we lead. Becoming conscious of this reality (or of anything else) requires stopping long enough to receive the information. It is in this silence that we are able to reflect. As I've mentioned before, solitude does not come often for most of us unless we intentionally create it. So regularly making time in which you can be still and silent becomes an important part of overall wellness. These moments help you connect with yourself so that you can become aware of how you've been focusing on certain areas in life and not focusing on others.

We have to consciously give this some thought to recognize what our choices have been. One available time to do this might occur upon waking up in the morning, or when you're lying in bed at night. This is (hopefully) a relaxed moment to review the past day or days and decide how you would like the immediate future to be shaped. We also could do this when we go for a walk, sit quietly or before or after meditating.

The equilibrium we are seeking fits in with the principles of Chinese Medicine. These principles are based on balancing the polarities of life that exist within the body and outside of the body. There is a constant shifting between two opposing forces like light and dark, yin and yang, masculine and feminine, cold and hot, wet and dry, etc. It is the same within our own lives; these dualities are in and around us all the time and our life works by going back and forth between them. When we can find the middle ground, the balancing point, is when human beings thrive the most.

When I was studying to be a wellness coach through Coaches Training Institute, we looked at balancing areas of our life as if they were (equal) pieces of a pie. The areas we used were Career, Money, Fun and Recreation, Health, Friends and Family, Significant Other/Romance, Personal Growth and Physical Environment. The point was to look at each area and rank your level of satisfaction with each life area by using a number one through ten. This helps you see the big picture in terms of where you put your energy, and also helps you make decisions about how you would like things to shift so that you can live a more balanced life.

When we are in big life transitions such as starting a new career or having a major health issue, one area demands a huge amount of attention for a period of time while other areas become out of balance. When a person is dealing with cancer for example, his or her work life will probably get less attention as the main focus becomes his or her health, personal growth and being in a positive environment. This situation will not last indefinitely. There will come a point when the focus on the illness or on a "new" job or career will lessen to make room for re-balancing the other areas in your life.

Although we all have seasons where we lose our balance, there are benefits in attempting to approach our lives in a balanced way. When we are feeling more balanced we are more likely to bring forth our best selves. Other benefits include being more efficient and effective in the activities that we are involved in and feeling deep satisfaction and joy with the way we are living. This can give us a greater ability to deepen our relationships with the people we care about and increase an overall acceptance of ourselves and the lives we lead.

Questions to explore life balance

1) If you made your own 8 or 10-part wheel, what areas would you include?

2) When you give a number 1 through 10 to rate your satisfaction with the amount of attention you give to each area, what do you find?

3) Do you feel that your life is fairly balanced right now or out of balance?

4) If you're out of balance, what areas seem to be where you spend most of your time? and what areas do you spend little or no time on?

5) Can you see how this imbalance is affecting your life as a whole?

6) Is there something that is necessary but temporarily causing an imbalance in your life?

7) Are there any changes you would like to make immediately having looked at it this way?

8) Are there bigger changes you would like to make for some long-term balance in your life?

"Do not grow old, no matter how long you live. Never cease to stand like curious children before the Great Mystery into which we were born."

— *Albert Einstein*

Chapter 15

Where to Go from Here

The journey of health and healing has just begun for some of you. For others, this book has been a resource to help you continue on your journey with new inspiration. It is time to integrate the information in this book in a way that speaks to you, and more importantly, to confront the information that is difficult to face. All of you will go about this in different ways, and hopefully with a new sense of love and respect for all parts of yourself, your body, mind and spirit.

We value our diversity as people and yet we all have many of the same needs. So as you continue on with this act of love, remember that I and many others share this journey with you. You are not alone, and although changing some aspects of your lifestyle is not always easy, you will be grateful for your efforts. So will your children, friends and all of your loved ones.

My hope is that you take away from this book many new ideas that get you excited and motivated to make changes about your health. If you haven't taken the time yet to go through the questions included in the chapters, you may wish to go back and reflect on one set of questions at a time. The insights they provide will make your personal journey much more clear for you. The process of healing any aspect of our being is also a process of self-knowing. When we become conscious of how we think, feel, and behave in the world we can then accept "what is" and make the changes we choose that will most benefit our body, mind and spirit. Living with compassion for ourselves and others will bring us greater understanding, acceptance and love for ourselves and life in general. It also provides us with enthusiasm for improving our lives. This process of learning never stops and continuing to consciously grow and heal is a beautiful way toward a rich, fulfilling and vibrant life.

Bibliography
for Energy Medicine Related Books

Borysenko, J. PhD. (1994). *The Power of the Mind to Heal.* Carson, CA: Hay House, Inc.

Brennan, B. (1987). *Hands of Light: A Guide to Healing Through the Human Energy Field.* New York, NY: Bantam Books. (A NASA physicist who could see energy as a child. Includes scientific basis of energy healing and great illustrations of the human energy system.)

Brennan, B. (1993). *Light Emerging: The Journey of Personal Healing.* New York, NY: Bantam Books.

Bruyere, R. L. (1989 5th printing 1993). *Wheels of Light.* Arcadia CA: Bon Productions.

Chopra, D. M.D. (1990). *Quantum Healing.* New York, NY: Bantam Books.

Dossey, L .M.D. (1999). *Reinventing Medicine.* New York: Harper Collins.

Gerber, R. MD. (1988). *Vibrational Medicine: New Choices for Healing Ourselves.* Sante Fe, New Mexico: Bear & Company.

Hover-Kramer, D. (2002). *Healing touch: A Guidebook for Practitioners.* Albany, NY: Delmar. (written by nurses) includes research of Healing Touch

Judith, A. (1987) and (1999). *Wheels of Life: A User's Guide to the Chakra System.* Woodbury, MN: Llewellyn Publications.

Lipton, B. PhD. (2005). *The Biology of Belief.* Santa Rosa CA: Mountain of Love/Elite Books.

Oschman, J. L. (2000). *Energy Medicine: The Scientific Basis.* NY: Churchill Livingstone. Servan-Schreiber, D. M.D. PhD. (2008). *Anti-Cancer - A New Way of Life.* New York, NY: Viking Penguin.